Creative Thinking

evolve or die

Creative Thinking:
A Field Guide to Building Your Strategic Core

Dr. Angus Fletcher, PhD
Professor, The Ohio State University

for
US Army
Command & General Staff College

In Memoriam, Colonel Scott Green

> *ignem non moriatur*
> the fire never dies

War breaks victory's old rules. . .
Genius creates the new.
—Carl von Clausewitz

Mission Statement

The goal of this Field Guide is to provide you, the US Army's officers and advanced enlisted personnel, with a bootstrap guide that you can use to train yourself to be more creative.

Why be more creative? Because creativity is the human brain's power to adapt to fast-changing, life-and-death environments, overcoming emergent challenges and leveraging emergent opportunities. It's what enabled our species to thrive in the chaotic and uncertain ecosystems of evolution by natural selection. It makes us antifragile in situations where computer AI turns brittle, and it will allow you to outcompete and win in volatile, unstable domains.

To make this Guide as user-friendly as possible, it's not written in science-speak or techno-jargon. It's written in stories that have been scientifically-developed to directly activate your brain's deep creative centers. So, you don't need to understand the neuroscience to get all the benefits. Just read the stories and enjoy, trusting the work of your subconscious brain.

The Guide is organized into major sections, of escalating build:

- Section One focuses on developing your *emotional desire* to be creative, because this desire is the source of innovation.
- Section Two focuses on unlocking your brain's innate creativity by down-powering logic and up-powering narrative cognition (or more colloquially, storythinking.)
- Section Three provides starter techniques (like prioritizing exceptional information) for boosting your natural creativity.
- Section Four provides games and exercises for practicing creativity. That's because creativity training is like physical training. Creativity is a muscle in your brain that has to be strengthened through regular exercise so that it's strong when you need it. To make training stick, it has to be fun and engaging, prompting you to incorporate it aggressively into your daily routine.
- Section Five provides some more advanced techniques, such as how to translate creativity into innovation.

4

To incorporate scientific rigor, the Guide contains several sets of definitions along with a formal review of equations at the end. There's also a quick reference in the form of "10 Myths About Creativity," that solidifies the underlying scientific precepts.

This Guide is based on a groundbreaking new science of creativity, pioneered at Ohio State's Project Narrative, in conjunction with teams at UPenn Psychology, USC's Brain and Creativity Institute, and UChicago's Polsky Center for Entrepreneurship and Innovation. The new science is rooted in psychology, so it's mutually reinforcing with current techniques from sports psychology, etc., for developing resilience. Resilience breeds confidence and optimism, which support creative thinking, which in turn produces positive outcomes that boost confidence and optimism, feeding resilience. The new science of creativity also emphasizes perspective-taking, situational openness, and cooperative teamwork, making it a strong match for anyone who wants to harness individual freedom and diversity in a controlled and disciplined manner for the public good.

This Guide is meant as a Creative Thinking 101. So, like a Biology 101 textbook, it will ground you in the big foundations. But it's only about one-percent of what we know. So, if you have questions or want greater detail, there's plenty more to fill your brain.

—CGSC, July 2021

Table of Contents

Definitions

Creativity: Plotting original actions.

Tactics: Creativity in response to local threats and opportunities.

Strategy: Creativity in response to global threats and opportunities.

Innovation: A tactic or strategy that succeeds.

Compliance: Innovation, institutionalized.

War: The competitive destruction of compliance, forcing further innovation.

The Simple Dirty

You were born creative.

But to win, you must get more creative.

To get more creative, you must think outside your perspective.

To think outside, you must forget what *has* worked and seek what *can*.

To seek what can work, you must dismiss your hopes and fears.

You must embrace the strange, the unexpected, the exceptional.

You must get in the habit of planning fast and re-planning faster.

You must forget about being perfect and strive only to get better.

You must have many minds inside, including your enemy's mind.

You must see defeat as a chance to plan again.

And above all, you must have courage.

Courage is trying new things.

Courage is attacking the unknown.

Courage is becoming a different person.

Courage is innovation's root.

With it, you will adapt and overcome.

Introduction

You've just hit the beachhead when you discover: the enemy has been watching. He's learned all your protocols, your tactics, your secrets. He knows what you know, can think how you think, and is anticipating your every move. What do you do?

- You can overcome this shock—and every other shock in combat and beyond. All it takes is creative thinking.

- Creative thinking makes you adaptive, resilient, unpredictable, So that even when you're surprised, you're prepared. Even in chaos, you advance with purpose. Even in calamity, you win.

- To train up your creativity, read this book in order, module by module. Don't rush or skip ahead. You'll gain more by mastering a few modules deeply than by flicking through all the modules superficially.

- Each module contains exercises, and they're called exercises for a reason: the more you repeat them, the more they'll strengthen you. So, repeat them, over and over, for life.

- Enjoy the training. There's nothing more gratifying than being creative.

Section One: Want It, Get It

- The first step to doing anything is to _want_ to do it.

- To get strong, you must _want_ to train your body.

- To get disciplined, you must _want_ to drill your mind.

- To get creative, you must _want_ to be creative. And the more you want it, the more you'll get it.

- So, this section will deepen your desire to get creative.

- You will learn that creative thinking is the secret to who you are and what makes your life a gift to others.

- You will discover that creative thinking provides the chance to rewrite destiny and wrest triumph from defeat, rising above the challenges of the day to invent a better world— and become your better self.

Module 1: Born to Innovate

You were born to innovate. The proof lies in your ancestors.

Your first ancestor is life. Life emerged 3.5 billion years ago, and it birthed evolution, filling the world with new creations.

Your second ancestor is action. Action evolved 2 billion years ago. At first, action was blind, a propeller-whip that pulsed at random frequencies. But then action learned to respond to feedback, enabling adaptation.

Your third ancestor is thought. Thought evolved 600 million years ago in the neuron, which made possible planning, perspective-taking, and the other tools of imagination.

These three ancestors came together 300,000 years ago to make the human brain, a life that can think up endless new actions. The human brain is mediocre at logic and information processing. Which is why math is hard and why computers beat you at crunching data. But the human brain's threefold inheritance of evolution, adaptation, and imagination have made it the undisputed champion of innovation, allowing it to create the wonders of art and technology that now crowd our globe.

That gift of practical creativity runs through your family tree. Your forefathers and foremothers innovated farming, medicine, cooking, business, carpentry, and more. Go back ten generations in your family, you'll find a dozen innovators; go back a hundred, you'll find a Sun Tzu, da Vinci, Cleopatra, Shakespeare, Shaka Zulu, Einstein, Genghis Kahn, Florence Nightingale, Maya Angelou, or Clausewitz.

Their spirit of innovation lives on in you. But it will only show itself in full if you have bravery.

The bravery to be individual.

The bravery to fail in public.

The bravery to retain your optimism in defeat.

The bravery to challenge the pack.

The bravery to change your mind.

The bravery to embrace uncertainty.

The bravery to do what your ancestors did.

The bravery to risk what no one else has ever risked before.

Exercise 1. Identify a member of your family tree who did something new, original, utterly individual. Commemorate their achievement by writing a one-page biography.

Exercise 2. Recall a time in your childhood when you had the courage to split from the crowd and go your own way. Find that youthful maverick in you now. List three things that maverick would do in your job, today.

Module 2: War's Great Unknown

The professors of the eighteenth century believed that every battle was won the night before.

The professors were the products of the Age of Reason. And Reason taught that life was a machine that obeyed mathematical laws. Those laws predetermined everything. Know them, and you could compute victory before a shot was fired.

As the nineteenth century dawned, this theory seemed proved by the ascendance of Napoleon. Napoleon was a paragon of Reason. He instituted math and physics in schools across Paris. He reformed France's tangled judicial system into a systematic Legal Code. And in battle after battle—Ulm, Austerlitz, Friedland—he wielded logic to crush Europe's mightiest armies and savviest generals. Thanks to Napoleon's invincible foresight, victory was never in doubt.

But then suddenly, Reason collapsed. In 1812, Napoleon catastrophically miscalculated his invasion of Russia, squandering a seemingly unbeatable force of half-a-million men. Then in 1815, he was routed at Waterloo. And in the aftermath of that disaster, a thirty-something Prussian colonel by the name of Carl von Clausewitz, who'd retired from active calvary service to direct the War Academy in Berlin, drew the conclusion that the professors of Reason had got it wrong. There was no way to win a war in advance. War was fog and friction. And fog and friction destroyed the best-laid plans.

So radical was this new theory of war that Clausewitz did not risk publishing it in his own lifetime. So radical was this new theory of war that it was ignored at 1850s West Point, where the officers who'd later witness the muddled butchery of Gettysburg were trained to believe that battles could be won with clockwork precision. So radical was this new theory of war that it still appears radical today.

Today we live in an even greater Age of Reason. Today we have computer Artificial Intelligence that claims to predict the future. Today we have endless metrics and spreadsheets for making failsafe, data-driven decisions. Today we have Power Points, acronyms, standard operating procedures, and a million other surefire formulas for success.

But what was true at Waterloo and Gettysburg remains true now. There is no way to program victory. If you're fighting anywhere except a digital simulation, environmental friction and fog will frustrate your plans. And a human adversary, born and bred in cultures different from your own, will shatter them irreparably.

This is why no plan has ever survived, or will ever survive, war. War is, by its essence, the breakdown of order. It is the limit edge of civilization, the release of nature's primal chaos back into our tidy datapoints and equations. If you hew religiously to the plan you made last night, today's battle will demolish you.

But, take heart. Be excited, optimistic, and bold. Because even though war destroys plans, it doesn't destroy the planner. Quite the opposite: war _unleashes_ the planner. The planner revels in times of unpredictable change, because in those times, there's always a new plan to be created.

That's why Napoleon was never really a successful forecaster. In victory, he was always an improvisor, an adaptor, a creative thinker. As he put it: _L'imagination gouverne le monde_—"Imagination rules the world."

And that's why you will win, too. Because you will plan before battle, not to have a plan—but to practice planning. That practice will energize your innate creativity, giving you the confidence to plan and plan again.

So you react with imagination to achieve your mission in the maelstrom.

Exercise 1.   Identify moments of chaos in the day. Notice how chaos can bring out other people's worst—panic, anger, blame—but your best: courage, ingenuity, care.

Exercise 2.   Dwight Eisenhower once remarked: "In preparing for battle, I have always found that plans are useless, but planning is indispensable." Recall a past plan of yours that failed. Then write out how you rebounded from that failure by planning again.

Module 3: Creativity Complements Compliance

It's early September 1862 at Harper's Ferry, a ramshackle town surrounded by a high plateau, a higher peak, and an even higher ridge. Those heights make the town virtually indefensible, but even so, the town must be defended: it guards a railroad bridge across the Potomac, carrying vital coal supplies to Union factories churning out the armaments the North needs to win the Civil War.

The North has therefore garrisoned the town with 12,500 soldiers, under the command of Colonel Dixon Miles. Miles is a West Point graduate who was twice cited for "gallant" conduct during the Mexican-American War but who has more recently disgraced himself at the First Battle of Bull Run getting drunk out of a mix of boredom and resentment at being assigned to the reserves. Harper's Ferry is his chance to redeem himself, and his orders are clear: "Hold the town."

Serving under Miles is calvary officer Benjamin Franklin "Grimes" Davis. Grimes is another West Point grad, but he's twenty-five years younger than Miles and has less than half the combat experience. His unit is a motley crew of New York, Illinois, Maryland, Rhode Island, and Virginia riders. And making him even more suspect in the eyes of his commanding officers is the fact that he's a southerner: born in Alabama and raised in Mississippi, three of his younger brothers are now fighting for the Confederates under Robert E. Lee. His orders are also clear: "Do what Colonel Miles tells you."

All is well in the town——until September 11, when a frightened brigade of Northern troops unexpectedly appears. The troops explain that they're being hounded by a huge Southern army, maybe 25,000 rifles strong, with hundreds of cannon, led by the formidable Stonewall Jackson.

Consternation sweeps through Harper's Ferry. Battle is coming, probably the next day. There are only a few precious hours of daylight to prepare.

But what should that preparation be? Grimes and several other junior officers urge Miles to take the offensive, dispatching troops to occupy the three heights and unleashing calvary to ambush Jackson's artillery. Miles, however, rejects this as a breach of his orders to station his forces at Harper's Ferry. He has not been told to "Occupy the heights" or "Ambush the enemy." He has been told to "Hold the town," and dammit, he will follow that command. Dismayed by Miles's attitude of unimaginative compliance, Grimes protests that there's no way to "Hold the town" if the enemy gets his cannon on the slopes above. But Miles, not wanting to be chastised again by his superiors, insists on hunkering obediently in place.

The next day, Stonewall Jackson arrives at Harper's Ferry. And he is amazed to discover that the plateau above the town is barely guarded—and that the heights to the south and west aren't guarded at all. Seizing the chance, he orders his soldiers to grab the heights, and by September 14, they have begun hauling up four enormous Parrot Rifles and four-dozen other pieces of artillery to bombard the town. Realizing the catastrophe that is about to ensue, Grimes demands that he be allowed to lead his calvary on a break out. Miles rejects this as a violation of his orders to "Hold the town" and instead dispatches a courier across South Mountain to his own commanding officer, General McClellan, asking for permission to surrender.

General McClellan is appalled by Miles' request. He orders Miles not to surrender but to assault the heights. Yet the order never makes it to Miles, who continues to sit compliantly in Harper's Ferry, as his helpless Union army is targeted by Jackson's heavy guns.

In the meantime, Grimes defies Miles and gallops out of the surrounded town on a pontoon bridge—after which, he manages to ambush more than forty ordinance wagons, delivering McClellan his first major calvary victory. While back in Harper's Ferry, cannonballs are falling, killing Miles and forcing his 12,000 troops to surrender—the largest capture of Union soldiers in the entire war.

Those are the basic facts about the Battle of Harper's Ferry. Now here's the question: Who better served his commanding officer? Miles, who followed his orders literally? Or Grimes, who followed their deeper spirit?

To McClellan, the answer was obvious: Grimes. And the same answer remains obvious to the Army's generals today. General Mark Milley, appointed Chairman of the Joint Chiefs in 2019, has asked us to imagine that he's just told a young officer to destroy the enemy by seizing Hill 101. But then. . .

. . . the young officer sees Hill 101, and the enemy is over on Hill 102. What does he do? Does he do what I told him to do, seize Hill 101? Or does he achieve the purpose, destroy the enemy on Hill 102?

The answer is: Do what Grimes would do. Seize Hill 102.

That's because creative thinking isn't the enemy of compliance. It's the *source* of compliance. It's what invented the current regulations. It's why those regulations work.

So, as long as those regulations are working, keep creativity in reserve. But when the rules begin to buckle from the unforeseen, activate your creativity to preserve your institution's deep intent.

Honoring the rules by reinventing them.

Exercise 1.   Write down two or three of your unbreakable life rules. Then identify the deeper purpose beneath each rule. And imagine a situation where you'd need to bend or even break the rule to preserve its fundamental intent.

Exercise 2.   Identify one of your unit's operational rules of action—then imagine a situation where you'd need to adapt the rule in order to preserve its greater spirit.

Module 4: Win This Battle, Not the Last One

It was 19 October 202 BC, upon the dusty plains of Zama. To the northwest were the graying remnants of Rome's Fifth and Sixth Legions, exiled for their humiliating defeat to a Carthaginian general at the Battle of Cannae, fourteen years before. And waiting across the battlefield, to the southeast, was that same Carthaginian general: Hannibal.

Hannibal was sure that he'd humiliate the legions again. After all, he hadn't just humiliated them at Cannae. He'd humiliated them at Ticinus, Trebia, Lake Trasimene, and Geronium. And he'd done so every time with the same basic tactic: unpredictable movement. Deploying light calvary, fast skirmishers, and galloping cattle with their horns ablaze, Hannibal had disorientated the Romans, neutralizing their great technological advantage: heavy infantry. Before Hannibal, that infantry had mown down army after army, defeating Samnites, then Gauls, then Western Greeks. But it had been scrambled by Hannibal's irregular attacks, turned lumbering, confused, and flatfooted like a rhinoceros mobbed by bees.

To repeat his winning tactic, Hannibal had come to Zama with a horde of the ultimate chaos inciters: war elephants. Those beasts had struck terror into Rome's soldiers in previous battles. So, certain that they'd cause panic again, Hannibal had assembled eighty of the long-trunked animals, their tusks gleaming eerily. And with a self-assured gesture, Hannibal began the day's fight by ordering the monsters forward.

His breezy confidence was undone by what happened next. For instead of bolting in fear, the Romans pulled a Hannibal: they initiated their own unpredictable movement. Their forward line parted, creating gaps that the elephants plodded into, before being lanced to death by pilum-wielding legionaries.

The Romans had evolved. They weren't the old Romans that Hannibal had defeated earlier. They had transformed into agile movers. And they now moved agilely to destroy Hannibal, routing him into exile.

Hannibal's disaster is the disaster that befalls every commander who prioritizes what *has* worked over what *can* work. That's because knowledge of what has worked comes from the past. And if you focus on the past, you will always be fighting the last war—dooming you to be outflanked by an adversary who's imagining the next one.

So, if you want to win the victory, remember: your enemy has already mastered your previous moves. To defeat him, you must reinvent yourself.

You must stop being a product of history. And you must make the future a product of yourself.

Exercise 1.   Pick a historical war. Study its first major battle and its last, noting the evolution of weapons and tactics. Speculate on what would happen if the war's first battle was fought with the weapons and tactics of the last.

Exercise 2.   Identify a core tool or tactic in your arsenal. Now imagine that it has suddenly become obsolete. Speculate on what has neutralized it. And then imagine a counter to that new development.

Module 5: Creativity is Your Gift to Others

"Don't kill anybody. And don't lose an airplane."

This was the order given to 33-year-old Lieutenant Commander Dan Pedersen in December 1968 when he was tasked with founding a new fighter school at the Navy's Miramar Air Station, on a seaside mesa outside San Diego.

The order was issued with the best intentions. The Navy was hemorrhaging pilots and aircraft over the jungles of Vietnam in Operation Rolling Thunder, and it was convinced that its shocking casualties were due to the high failure rate of its F-4 Phantoms' air-to-air missiles. To fix the glitch, Admiral Tom Moorer, Chief of Naval Operations, had therefore commissioned an in-depth study——the Ault Report——that devoted 200 pages to detailing how missile performance could be upgraded. This report was the source of the order issued to Petersen: tucked into the small print of the document's hefty paperwork, as item 11 of 15 under paragraph 6 on page 37, was a recommendation to establish an Advanced Fighter Weapons School that taught pilots how to best finesse the buggy missiles.

The admiralty's position was thus crystal clear: pilots were dying because of substandard compliance. Missiles had been rushed into service too fast and now the whole process had to be slowed down and troubleshot carefully. The manufacturing and supply chain needed to be brought up to code. The pilots had to be drilled rigorously in the missiles' technical specs. And to ensure that no more lives were sacrificed to the overaggressive decision-making that had got the faulty missiles greenlit in the first place, Pedersen's main job was to enforce the rules, adhering to established safety guidelines and doing everything possible to reduce risk.

In other words: "Don't kill anybody. And don't lose an airplane."

But Pedersen thought different. He thought the real reason that pilots were dying was that they were already _too_ rule-bound. They flew robotically, sticking rigidly to textbook laws of tactics that had been derived to apply to all aircraft, from biplanes to bombers. This unimaginative choreography had been detected by the enemy, who had cannily memorized the US pilots' predictable dogfight patterns. The result was slaughter in the sky, as rote-flying F-4 Phantoms were shot down by a nimble adversary that had hacked the Americans' drone-like decision-making.

So, to give his pilots a fighting chance, Pedersen decided to buck his orders and get creative. He tossed away the textbook tactics and instructed his pilots on the individual particulars of the enemy's actual planes. He warned that every adversary was unique and every fight asymmetric. And he staffed his new school with instructors like John "Smash" Nash, whose main advice to students was: "Automobiles, aircraft, and air-to-air missiles are built to fail. Expect problems and anticipate them." Where the Navy's leadership was attempting to build more trustworthy missiles, Pedersen thus pivoted in the opposite direction. He wanted his pilots to always *distrust* their equipment, treating failure as routine.

This new curriculum produced a radical shift of mindset. The old mindset had been to cautiously avoid death in training. The new mindset was to aggressively _embrace_ death in training, forcing pilots to confront all the ways they could die in the sky. Rather than obeying rules out of timid self-preservation, Pedersen's pilots bravely opened their minds to everything that could go sideways in combat, so that when the unexpected struck, they were psychologically prepared to adapt and overcome.

Pedersen's innovative training regime yielded spectacular benefits: the success rate of US Navy pilots climbed 500%, while the Air Force, which had responded to the Ault Report by upgrading its weapon systems, suffered an increase of pilot deaths. Pederson became a hero and his training regime became a legend, immortalized in Hollywood's *Top Gun* and implemented across the military at hubs such as the US Army's National Simulation Center. Where risk-avoidance had sacrificed lives, Pedersen's creativity had saved them.

That's the power of creativity. When the old system breaks down, when the existing procedure traps you in a dead end, when the pre-programmed textbook maneuver walks you into an ambush, creativity can not only provide an escape route but hand you back the initiative, enabling you to do what Dan Pedersen did and actively protect the people who depend upon you.

And creativity can save lives in other ways. It can shatter stalemates and win battles faster, bringing violence to a quicker end. It can even help avoid violence entirely; discovering inventive ways to resolve conflict without resorting to force.

And finally, by daring to be creative, you can do what the heroes of 1776 did for Dan Pedersen and what Pedersen then did for his students: inspire them to be revolutionaries, too. Through your example, you can pass on the gift of innovation to future generations, sparking them to discover the power within.

The power to make a new future for everyone.

Exercise 1.   Identify a teaching or a tool that's improved—and maybe even saved—your life. Research the history of its creation. Record the moments of imagination that went into its development.

Exercise 2.   Identify a hero who had the courage to do something innovative. Then imagine yourself as that hero. Imagine how that hero might overcome a stalemate in your life—or improve an underperforming feature of your work area.

Module 6: If You Want To Become More Creative, You Will

The sky spread wide and blue when Julius Caesar heard the news.

It was September 52 BC in central Gaul, and Caesar's legions were constructing a ten-mile siege wall around the hilltop ramparts of Alesia. Inside sat Vercingetorix, a Gallic chieftain of such military charisma that he'd united Gaul's infighting clans into a single army, half-a-million warriors strong. He had 80,000 of those tall, long-sworded warriors with him now, almost double the number of Caesar's legions.

Those legions weren't worried, despite their smaller numbers. They were better equipped and trained than the Gauls. And they knew that the Gauls were only a threat when in the open. In the open, the Gauls could deploy their lightning calvary and irregular attack patterns to rattle and outflank the Romans. But Caesar, with his usual brilliance, had shut down that possibility. The Gauls were trapped inside the siege wall, and the wall was unbreakable. It loomed twelve-feet high, ringed with battlements, surrounded by trenchworks, and buttressed by towers. Slowly, it would strangle Vercingetorix until he had no choice other than to capitulate—or dash himself to bits against Rome's superior engineering.

But then the news came: Vercingetorix had sent for the rest of his army. And it had answered his call, rumbling toward Caesar with vast numbers of long-sworded warriors, chariots, and horsemen. It was now the Romans who were encircled. And as the legionaries blinked through the cold, September rain, they realized that the Gauls had set a trap, pretending to sit still when they were really catching Caesar in a massive pincer.

The only logical thing for the Romans to do now was flee. If they moved fast, abandoning their siege wall, they could save themselves from being overrun from behind. It would be a humiliating retreat, certainly. It would tarnish Caesar's reputation, perhaps forever. But what else could you do when you'd been surrounded by an army that outnumbered you ten to one?

These were the sensible thoughts that echoed through the minds of Caesar's officers. And Caesar felt them in his mind as well. But then he looked up, through the day's gathering mist, at the wide, blue sky above. And he saw another possibility. He would not run. He would build a second ten-mile wall, around the first, but facing in the opposite direction. That second wall would enable the Romans to fight a two-front siege, choking Vercingetorix in Alesia while they held off the Gallic reinforcements from beyond.

When Caesar presented this plan to his legions, they blinked, agog. No such battleplan had ever been attempted. Indeed, no such battleplan had ever been *imagined.* It violated all the rules of traditional siege warfare—and contravened the most fundamental law of combat. That law was to avoid being attacked on both sides at once. Yet now, here was Caesar, flaunting that law. Instead of breaking the enemy's pincer, he was inviting it. The Romans would literally build their own coffin, trapping themselves in the narrow gap between two wooden walls.

But impossibly, the walls worked. Caesar galloped up and down the channel between, rallying his legions to defeat the Gaulish berserkers and capture Vercingetorix. It was the most astonishingly inventive victory in the history of the legions, and when news of Caesar's unthinkable triumph reached Rome, even his Senate rivals were awestruck. Unable to deny his achievement, they ordered a festival that filled 20 nights with song.

As later generations have looked back in equal amazement at Caesar's boldly original tactic, they have asked: *How did he imagine that double wall? What gave him the vision—and the courage—to so totally defy conventional wisdom?*

The answer is disarmingly simple: Caesar was unique because he _wanted_ to be unique. Even in his teenage years, long before he had any combat experience, he consciously—even antagonistically— flouted the status quo. The status quo was for Roman men to wear short sleeves and tight belts, so young Caesar stepped out in public in long sleeves, loose belted. For this fashion outrage, he was mocked across Rome for looking like an effeminate slave. But he continued wearing his unorthodox clothes. Which is to say: *He made an intentional choice to stand out.* And the more that he chose to stand out, the more that he did. He intentionally made himself an original.

Other imaginative commanders have done the same. Alexander the Great defied the sartorial standards of the Macedonian court by adopting the attire of Persian kings—and then defied the sartorial standards of the Persian kings by blending them with Macedonian garb, ushering in his own uniquely imperial chic. Napoleon stuck out by opting for the opposite tactic: in an era where French officers glammed up like peacocks, he cultivated an insistently unglamorous look. At the time of his Italian campaign, he wore his hair in a square, dogeared bob that contemporaries described as "a most peculiar fashion." And as he ascended to emperor, he continued his approach of being the most underdressed man in the room, favoring a colonel's coat among his generals.

This intentionally individual attire can seem a waste of energy. What does it matter how a commander dresses? Surely, true geniuses focus on their plans not their wardrobes. But modern neuroscientific research has demonstrated the opposite. That research has shown that the single biggest factor in increasing creativity is the _desire_ to be original. The more actively that you want to think and act differently, the more that you will.

This doesn't mean that you have to make a splash by dressing as idiosyncratically as Caesar, Alexander, and Napoleon. But it does mean that you have to dedicate yourself to being creative. Press yourself, aggressively and insistently, to think up new and better ways of executing your daily routine. Challenge yourself to improve on old standbys. Identify strongly as an innovator.

That identification comes easier to some people; Caesar almost certainly felt instinctively inclined to break the mold. To you, it might feel less natural. And even if you have an inborn disposition to walk your own way, the social pushback you experience might make you wonder whether conscious originality isn't just pretentious and attention-seeking.

But the choice to be creative is worth making. That's because life's most necessary and altruistic act is inventive leadership. Inventive leadership wins victories and saves lives. So, give that gift to others by having the courage to consciously innovate the norm. Be your own Caesar and bend the course of history by committing yourself to being what every great commander is: an individual, an independent thinker, an original.

Exercise 1. Write out a list of the most important people in your life. Beside each name, note something utterly unique about that person, something that cannot be duplicated or replaced. Then commit yourself to supporting and protecting that special quality by being equally special yourself.

Exercise 2. Alexander the Great intentionally cultivated his creativity by writing epic poetry; Caesar, by writing plays; Napoleon, by writing a novel. Imagine your own novel or film about a future military commander—what would make that commander unprecedented, revolutionary, unique?

Section Two: Unlock Your Creativity

- In this section, we'll transition from creativity's emotional *why* into its practical *how*.
- The first step toward that *how* is learning to access the natural creativity already inside you.

Definitions

Logic:	Using induction and deduction to perform evidence-based reasoning, critical thinking, mathematics, and interpretation.
Causal Reasoning:	Using speculation to link causes to effects, actions to outcomes, actors to events.
Plotting:	A synonym for causal reasoning. Aka, thinking in narratives, or planning and strategizing.
Induction:	Deriving general rules from all available datapoints. How machine-learning algorithms work.
Deduction:	Deriving new truths from general rules. How geometry works.
Speculation:	Hypothesizing new actions from a limited set of individual, often outlying, datapoints. How creative problem-solving works.

Module 7: Your Brain's Two Kinds of Smarts

In 1917, the US Army realized that it needed a way to gauge the smarts of would-be warfighters. So it developed the Alpha Test, a salvo of questions like:

A machine gun is more deadly than a rifle, because it

- *Was invented more recently*
- *Fires more rapidly*
- *Can be used with less training*

Over the ensuing decades, this test was improved into the Army General Classification Test, then the Armed Forces Qualification Test, and finally, the Armed Services Vocational Aptitude Battery or ASVAB.

The ASVAB has been administered to millions of recruits. And it has a proven track record of identifying intelligence. But as recent research in neuroscience has revealed, the ASVAB has a limit: it's designed to identify one kind of intelligence. And human brains possess two.

The first kind of intelligence is logic. Logic is the ability to perform evidenced-based reasoning, to think critically, to do mathematics, to interpret texts, and to perform other analytic, deductive, and computational tasks. It's also known as IQ; it's what's hardwired into computers; and it's what the ASVAB measures.

The second kind of intelligence is causal reasoning, aka plotting. It's the ability to speculate on causes and effects, to imagine narratives, to hypothesize experiments, to invent new technologies, and to generate original strategic and tactical plans. It's the source of innovation and adaptability—and it can't be performed by computers, which is why algorithms and AI become brittle in unstable, data-lean environments.

These two types of intelligence are complementary—but also fundamentally different. Logic is made of truths; plotting is made of actions. Logic is timeless; plotting is evolving. Logic is based on hard facts and reason; plotting is based on what scientists call hypothesis and what artists call imagination. Logic systematizes the past; plotting speculates on the future. Logic is certain and clarifying; plotting is flexible and empowering. Logic fosters compliance; plotting fosters creativity.

The reason that the ASVAB only measures the first type of intelligence is that until very recently, scientists believed that there <u>was</u> only one kind of intelligence: so-called "general intelligence." And that general intelligence, the scientists assumed, was logic. This is why almost all your coursework in high school and college stressed math, critical thinking, and other logic-based skills. And why the ASVAB does the same.

But now that scientists have identified the second type of intelligence, they have begun to identify how it works in the brain—and how to train up more of its power to invent innovative, game-changing actions. The basics of that training (along with a few advanced tips) will be outlined over the remaining pages of this book. But its foundation is the crucial scientific insight that creativity is driven in our brain by plotting, or in other words, by <u>thinking in story</u>. Thinking in story is the key to generating original plans, tactics, and strategies.

So, forget everything else you've been told about creativity and focus on getting better at plotting. Push your brain to imagine more original storylines and more individual story-characters, and in a short time you'll see the results: your brain's creative muscles will strengthen, cranking out more dynamic strategies and more revolutionary innovations.

The previous modules of this book filled your mind with stories—about the Battle of Zama, Top Gun, Harper's Ferry, and Alesia—and characters—Hannibal, Dan Pedersen, Napoleon, Caesar—to energize the plot-circuits of your imagination. And the following modules will now focus that mental energy via precise plotting techniques and technologies.

What traditional tests and schools have overlooked, and what even Clausewitz chalked up as ineffable genius, can be learned in an organized and methodical way. With hard work, discipline, and persistence, you can boost your brain's second kind of smart.

So, you don't just think logically. You also think *creatively*, going beyond ASVAB math and data to pass battle's adaptive test.

Exercise 1. To train yourself to identify the difference between logic and plotting, revisit one of your favorite narratives, whether in a novel, a film, or a history. Circle global events and character actions that make sense but aren't strictly rational. Your ability to process those events is evidence of your brain's powers of causal reasoning, or in other words, thinking in story.

Exercise 2. Write out the story of your past, sticking rigorously to the facts. Then write out three possible stories of your future, activating your brain's narrative circuitry to get creative.

Module 8: Shut Off Logic

Albert Einstein claimed he had a proven recipe for creativity: relaxing his brain. Sometime he relaxed it by playing his violin. Other times, by cruising about the open sea in his sailboat.

Vincent van Gogh and Ludwig Beethoven used versions of the same recipe. Only instead of playing a violin, van Gogh unwound by reading his favorite author: Shakespeare. And instead of cruising the open sea, Beethoven wandered the woods outside Vienna.

This counterintuitive recipe for creating great works has been confirmed by modern neuroscience. But modern neuroscience has also revealed that the recipe is a little different than Einstein thought. Because while it's true that Einstein, van Gogh, and Beethoven were relaxing their brain, they weren't relaxing *all* of their brain. They were relaxing one specific part: logic. And by relaxing that part, they freed the brain's other intelligence, plotting, to spring into action. They liberated their minds to launch into narrative adventures and conjectures.

Because creativity requires plotting, and because plotting is an active process, creativity cannot be achieved simply by relaxing. Creativity takes *work*, and a lot of it. That's why you can feel your brain slowly getting tired when you read stories, brainstorm ideas, or engage in other creative activities. You can only imagine for so long before your brain exhausts its creative muscles, requiring a break.

Over the next few modules, we'll explore how to sharpen and upgrade that imaginative work. But first, in this module, we'll lay the foundation for that work by focusing on how to relax logic. Logic, as we learned in the last module, operates in a fundamentally different way from plotting. So, the crucial first step toward maximizing your plotting potential is to actively shut down your brain's logical regions.

As Einstein, van Gogh, and Beethoven discovered, you can do this by rambling through nature, listening to music, or reading your favorite stories. But as modern science has revealed, there are also more targeted and efficient ways to power off your brain's logical circuits:

(1) Trade a perfection mindset for a satisfice approach, jettisoning your belief that there's a best or a right way to do something and instead embracing the knowledge that there are many equally good ways to get the job done. This mental technique is *pluralism*.

(2) Rather than defining what something _is_, imagine what it can _do_. So, instead of thinking, *That is an M8 smoke grenade*, think, *That can be used to signal, or conceal, or surprise, or distract, or. . .* This mental technique is *potential*.

(3) Treat data as a source of fresh ideas not as an obligation. Like you do with a book of quotes, focus on one datapoint that strikes you as particularly vivid or illuminating—and speculate on its bigger consequences. This mental technique is *inspiration*.

(4) Don't try to merge every detail or fact into a unified general conclusion. Instead, focus on what is distinct, unique, and special about each detail, so that rather than logically abstracting or blending, you emphasize the individuality of everything you observe. This mental technique is *exceptionalism*.

At first, these mental techniques might feel unnatural—even irresponsible or dangerous—to your logical mind. But by deploying these techniques, you're simply strengthening your creative circuits, not weakening your logical ones. Those logic circuits are just sitting on the sidelines, ready to be summoned when needed.

Which is to say: your overall training objective is to improve the performance of both the logical and the creative parts of your brain, so that you can fast-deploy each ability as appropriate. When compliance is crucial, you want to know exactly how creativity works, so you can keep it clear of the process. And when innovation is necessary, you want to know exactly how to pause logic, allowing you to quickly transition into an adaptive response.

Training yourself to pause logic takes as much discipline as training yourself to hone it. That's because you've been conditioned to prioritize critical thinking, evidence-based reasoning, and logic's other tools. And it's also because when you've relaxed in the past, you've done it like Einstein, Beethoven, and Van Gogh: instead of zeroing in specifically on relaxing logic, you've unwound in more imprecise ways.

So, it will take time and diligence to teach yourself to rapidly shut down your brain's logical processes—*without shutting down anything else*. But if you drill yourself on the four techniques above, focusing your mind on (1) pluralism, (2) potential, (3) inspiration, and (4) exceptionalism, you will isolate your brain's inner logic dial, giving you the power to crank it down or up on command.

Exercise 1.   Solve a work problem in three equally satisfactory ways.

Exercise 2.   Identify a tool in your workspace and then draft a list of all the things the tool could be used to do.

Exercise 3.   Pull a random book from your work library and skim its index, chapter titles, or section headings. Pick one that strikes your eye and use it to freestyle a new idea.

Exercise 4.   Make a list of the people on your team. Identify one unique way that each of their minds work.

Module 9: Story Constantly

In 1623, seven years after Shakespeare's death, his collected works were published in a massive folio book: it contained 36 original plays and stretched over 900 pages, almost two-thirds the length of the Bible.

As readers flicked through the book's seemingly endless table of contents—*Richard III*, *Romeo and Juliet*, *Henry 5*, *Much Ado About Nothing*, *Macbeth*, *Antony and Cleopatra*, *Othello*, *etc, etc, etc*—they drew a natural conclusion: the book's epic length was a product of Shakespeare's infinite imagination. Gifted with a boundless creativity, he'd poured out plots, crafting many more stories than the other playwrights of his generation.

But modern science has revealed that the reverse is true: Shakespeare didn't write so many stories because he was creative; he was creative because he wrote so many stories. This is why the youthful plays that Shakespeare wrote before he had much practice—*A Comedy of Errors*, *Henry 6*, *Titus Andronicus*—are his most formulaic, full of plot and character clichés taken from ancient books. And why his plays became increasingly innovative—*Hamlet*, *King Lear*, *The Tempest*—as he cranked out story after story, sometimes as many as three a year.

The same that goes for Shakespeare goes for other creative thinkers. They weren't born creative. They *became* creative by relentlessly exercising the plotting circuits of their brains.

Alexander the Great dreamed up narrative after narrative, imagining himself laying roads across Europe to the Pillar of Hercules, launching a vast naval invasion of Arabia, and even—in a flight of poetic imagination—conquering the moon. Leonardo da Vinci filled notebook after notebook with plans to invent flying engines, hand-cranked battle tanks, and crossbow gatling guns. Napoleon famously planned everything he did twice, advising his officers to do likewise: *Faire son thème en deux façons.*

These innovators all plotted relentlessly. They never regarded any plan as final; they re-scripted it constantly, through draft after draft, carrying multiple versions in their heads to account for potential exigencies. And they also actively initiated *new* plans. Instead of getting stuck on a single storyline that they revised over and over, they constantly hatched original schemes, until their minds were filled with a library of different stories of the future, each with its own rich subplots and branching variants. Like Shakespeare, they imagined hundreds of possible life stories, each as unique as Hamlet or Cleopatra.

If these creatives had attempted to act out all their inner plots and plans, they'd have descended into schizoid mania. But because this creative activity took place inside the brain, it was richly productive: it expanded Alexander, da Vinci, and Napoleon's ability to simultaneously inhabit multiple storylines—and multiple perspectives. Just like reiterated pullups strengthen a biceps, so did this repeated mental plotting strengthen the brain's creative muscle, giving it the power to craft richer, more elaborate strategies.

You can do the same for your brain's creative muscle by disciplining yourself to constantly expand your mental library of story. Story is another word for plot, which is another word for plan, which is another word for strategy. So, to become a more creative strategist. . .

- Dedicate yourself to improvising, expanding, and exploring original plotlines.
- Dedicate yourself to thinking from the perspective of different characters, so that like Shakespeare, you learn to plan not just like Henry 5 but also like Henry's adversaries—and his band of brothers.

You can practice these two skills every second of your life. Because your life is itself a story. Which means you're free to plot it. Start by planning original ways to spend your vacation time and weekends, then ramp up to imagining new ways to fulfill your responsibilities and job mandates. And don't just imagine how you would plan your time; imagine how people you respect would plan it.

And remember: just because you devise a plan, you don't have to execute it, so feel free to thought-experiment adventurously.

What's the most creative workday you can script? What innovation could you plot to make your organization its better self?

Exercise 1. What would you do if you were promoted into your superior's role? What new roles would you create within your team?

Exercise 2. Identify a workplan that you have high confidence in. Now imagine a second plan that is as detailed and as confidence inspiring.

Module 10: See Yourself As Part of a Bigger Narrative

Ulysses S. Grant had an irrational belief: "One of my superstitions [was] when I started to go anywhere, or do anything, not to turn back or to stop until the thing intended was accomplished."

So strong was this superstition that Grant would never, ever retrace his steps. If he realized that he was headed in the wrong direction, he would keep walking, down the road, until he hit another road that he could use to loop back. For miles, he would press on, illogically, because he was so sure that the gods smiled down on the persistent—and cursed those who retreated.

Grant wasn't the only successful leader with a weird belief in a greater power:

> Napoleon believed that he was watched over by a "little red man" who gave him glimpses of the future. *Don't invade Russia*, the little red man had whispered. And to Napoleon's eternal regret, he hadn't listened.

> Geronimo thought he a guardian spirit who bestowed him magical powers and warned him away from danger.

> The Red Baron had his lucky scarf, certain that it protected him—right up to the instant of his death.

These beliefs can seem absurd, even dangerous. What good can come of listening to mystic creatures or continuing down the wrong path? Yet they were all helpful. Not because miniature red prophets really exist. But because the beliefs of Grant, Napoleon, Geronimo, and the Red Baron all made them feel psychologically connected to a power bigger than themselves. And as modern neuroscience has shown, when our brain feels emotionally joined to a bigger power, it creates courage—and with it, optimism, resilience, and self-belief.

Those three qualities—optimism, resilience, and self-belief—are crucial for creativity. Creativity is choked by pessimism, defeatism, and doubt, which hijack our imagination with nay-saying and fear. So, if we want to adapt and overcome, it's crucial for us to believe that we *can* adapt and overcome. The moment we stop believing, our creativity stalls, and we spiral into fatalism.

That fatalism is deflected by superstitions and other magical beliefs that make us feel that we have a paranormal helper—like a lucky scarf—that can ward off disaster. So, as unscientific and untrue as superstitions are, they have the true, scientific effect of helping our brains adapt and overcome. That's why Geronimo was able to rebound from defeat, why the Red Baron was able to dogfight with such inventive grace, why Napoleon had the confidence to be a military original, and why Grant pressed forward on his Overland Campaign, through setback after setback—The Wilderness, Spotsylvania, North Anna, Cold Harbor—never retreating, until at last, he cornered the Confederate army at Petersburg, winning the Civil War.

But modern neuroscience has also shown that there's a more effective method for getting the psychological boost that Grant and the others got from their personal fairytales. That method is to tell our brain *true* stories about how innovation can save our lives. Or in other words, to connect our brain emotionally to a bigger narrative that's actually real.

To start with, remind your brain of the millions of innovations that have worked in the past, telling it the history of all the inventions that have turned the tide of nations and wars. Then retell the stories of all the times that you yourself have been successfully creative; those stories will strengthen your brain's emotional confidence that you can innovate again.

When your creativity fails, remember: even the most creative minds produce more misfires than masterpieces. The masterpieces will come, as long as you keep trying. And finally, know that creativity works better under pressure, so trust that as long as you keep practicing, it will be there when you really need it.

This belief in the power of innovation is true belief. Innovation will endure when lucky scarves fail and superstition breaks. Because innovation is the real story of life. Innovation is scientific fact, tried and tested, proved through billions of years of evolution. Innovation is what birthed our species and our civilization. And innovation is what is making our better future.

So, let go of fatalism and self-doubt. Have faith in your creative destiny—and you will adapt and overcome.

Exercise 1. Make a list of ten historical moments where an innovation in tactics or technology changed the balance of power, making an underdog into a victor.

Exercise 2. Revisit a moment in your past where you tried something new and it failed. Reimagine the moment in your mind, crafting a narrative of how it could have worked differently. Repeat that new narrative to yourself over the day.

Module 11: Plunge into the Unknown

In 512 BC, Sun Tzu was summoned by the king of Wu.

The king had read Sun Tzu's *Art of War* and was intrigued. But he was also wary. What if Sun Tzu was just a writer of books? What if Sun Tzu could tell fine stories about strategy but lacked the capacity to act strategically in real war? So, the king decided to test Sun Tzu.

"Can you command women?" The king asked Sun Tzu.

"Yes, my king."

"Then here is your army." The king clapped his hands, and into the court marched a harem, led by two concubines.

Without hesitation, Sun Tzu divided the women into two units, each commanded by one of the concubines. He armed each unit with spears. Then he struck up war drums, and ordered the women to march.

Instead, the women dissolved into laughter. And watching, the king began to laugh, too.

Calmly, Sun Tzu stopped the drums. He asked the two concubines: "Did your soldiers hear my orders?"

They smiled. "Yes."

"And did your soldiers understand them?"

They smiled again. "Yes."

"Then it was your job to enforce my orders. But you did not. You did not discipline your soldiers. So now, I must discipline you." And gesturing to the king's guards, he ordered them to behead the concubines.

The king stopped laughing. "Sun Zu! Do not kill those concubines! They are my favorite companions. Without them, my life will be joyless."

But Sun Tzu replied. "You have given me these soldiers, and I will command." So, to the king's horror, Sun Tzu again ordered the guards to behead the concubines. And the guards obeyed, decapitating the concubines before the king's eyes.

Turning his back on the bodies, Sun Tzu appointed two new women to lead the units, then struck up the drums. And this time, the units marched perfectly, just as Sun Tzu commanded.

Silencing the drums, Sun Tzu turned to the king. "My liege. Your army awaits you."

But the king was sickened by what he had seen, and he waved Sun Tzu away. "I have no interest in the army. Go home."

Sun Tzu did not go. Instead, he strode up to the king. And said wryly: "I see then that the king is just a reader of books. He likes fine stories about strategy, but does not have the stomach for it in real war."

Then the king acknowledged that Sun Tzu had passed the test. And he gave him the armies of Wu to command.

This is the only recorded story about Sun Tzu's life. And if you've heard it before, you were probably told that that it illustrates Sun Tzu's ruthless commitment to discipline. But really, it's proof of his creativity.

Sun Tzu had never commanded an army of concubines before. He did not know how they would react. And more importantly, he had not interacted with the king of Wu before. So, he did not know how the king would react. Sun Tzu was walking into an unprecedented situation, one that demanded creative thinking. And he responded with stunning originality, behaving in ways that violated social norms and shocked the king.

Sun Zu, in short, took a creative risk. He entered a new space and acted in a new way, inviting uncertainty. What if the king had been enraged by Sun Tzu's behavior and ordered him beheaded himself? What if the harem women had responded to the decapitation not by listening to Sun Tzu but by fleeing him? What if the guards ordered to behead the concubines had heeded the king and not Sun Tzu?

The answer is: It would not have mattered. It would not have mattered because Sun Tzu could have adapted to those plot twists—

—or to any others. He could have adapted because of the way he conducted himself from the beginning: he did not tentatively walk into the unfamiliar space of the king's palace, inching his way ahead. He entered aggressively, plunging into the unknown.

By doing so, he forced the members of the royal court to face what he had to face: uncertainty. His singular behavior shattered the palace's normal rules of operation, radically destabilizing the environment and instigating a unique situation that demanded a creative response. And he was confident that he could deliver that response faster than the king, the harem women, or anyone else.

Why was Sun Tzu confident? He was confident because he'd done it before. He'd practiced, again and again, throwing himself into wildly uncertain situations. When he'd initially begun that practice, he'd struggled, feeling panicky and overwhelmed. So, he knew that the king and the harem women were likely to struggle in the same way. They were used to the ordered protocols of the court, and this was their first taste of extreme volatility. It would therefore likely scare and disorient them, rendering them meek and docile.

And Sun Tzu also knew that, the more he'd practiced throwing himself into uncertainty, the better he'd done. He'd panicked less and adapted quicker. His powers of original action had improved.

That creative training is what made Sun Tzu confident. And that training, not his inflexible commitment to order, is what enabled him to the pass the king of Wu's test—and then to lead the king's armies to victory in future wars.

As it was for Sun Tzu, so too can it be for you. Prepare yourself to be creative on command by introducing uncertainty into your daily routine, gradually but intentionally, so that you increase your capacity for spontaneous inventiveness. Push yourself to enter new spaces and strike up conversations with strangers. Block clichéd small talk and mindless interpersonal routines; grow used to the discomfort of awkward pauses, leveraging adrenaline into heightened focus.

If you fail, congratulate yourself on attempting. If you succeed, push harder, challenging yourself to adapt on the fly.

Then when you enter an unprecedented life-or-death situation, welcome the unknown—and indeed, invite it. Actively generate the same breakdown of environmental order that Sun Tzu provoked in the palace of Wu, forcing your adversary to cope with escalating situational instability.

In that instability, you will stay calmer, create quicker, and adapt stronger. In that instability, you will innovate your way to victory.

Because that is how kings fall. And how strategists are made.

Exercise 1. Reach out to someone you admire but have never met. Schedule a meetup with them.

Exercise 2. Join a group or a team for an activity or a sport you've never done before.

Module 12: Actively Rest

George Washington was an avid dancer. He danced past midnight. He danced into his sixties. On 19 March 1779, deep in the middle of the Revolutionary War, he danced a three-hour marathon—without once sitting down—at Middlebrook, New Jersey, with the wife of his top general, Nathanael Greene.

And Washington didn't just dance. He danced intently and expertly. He was renowned for his minuet. And when his general staff expressed surprise that he devoted so much time to idle merriment, he replied that it was not merriment only. It was "the gentle conflict." Which was to say: dance was war without violence. What looked like empty play or routine choreography was a dynamic, serious contest. It was a competition, waged with a partner, to outdo other dancers—or one's own previous performance.

This cooperative battle made Washington a better general in many ways. One of which was nurturing his strategic imagination. That imagination, as we've seen over the previous modules, is a muscle strengthened by focused and enthusiastic exercise. But like every muscle, it does its real growing after workouts, during periods of rest.

Rest is crucial for your brain's creative regions. If you overwork them, you'll burn out, getting stuck in the same old ideas and feeling a funk of despair. When that happens, recharge your brain with a break. But before you take the break, know: some breaks are more effective than others.

The best breaks for your brain's creative regions are breaks that actively strengthen the parts of your heart and body that support creativity. The key parts of your heart are your positive emotions: optimism, empathy, curiosity, courage. And the key parts of your body are your physical athletics: cardiovascular, balance, strength.

So, now you know why dancing was such a healthy form of active rest for Washington. Dancing built strength in his limbs, balance in his torso, and cardiovascular pump in his chest. And it also bolstered his courage and optimism—and when done with a partner, his empathy and curiosity, all crucial elements of the neural perspective-taking that drives creativity.

But dancing isn't the only way to productively relax. When Washington was in camp, he exercised on horseback, another cooperative form of gentle conflict, this time against the hills and gullies of the East Coast landscape.

And if you don't have access to a nearby stallion, grab some other people to play a competitive team sport. Or, if you prefer solo sports such as running, recruit some runners to coach. That will ensure that the exercise grows not only your body but your heart.

To build creativity, you don't need to spend too much time actively resting. An hour a day is fine. (With an occasional three-hour marathon thrown in.) And if you want the most creative boost from your hour off, do it immediately after an intensive bout of creative thinking. When you follow focused creative work with active rest, you'll maximize the action of a brain region known as the default mode network. You'll feel it kicking into action if your mind starts wandering gently back to your creative problem while you're dancing, dribbling, or jogging.

Avoid artificial relaxants, such as alcohol. These can interfere with the emotional and physical wellbeing that supports creative thinking. If you want to shut off your brain entirely, unplug your life and go to sleep. Sleep is the most effective way to refresh your creativity.

And it even has its own built-in idea generator: dream.

Exercise 1. Focus all your attention for fifteen minutes on a problem that requires a creative solution. Then forget the problem and exercise hard for fifteen minutes. See what answers pop into your mind.

Exercise 2. Find someone in your unit who thinks differently from you. Then invite them to go rock climbing, sailing, or some other two-person dance-against-nature.

Exercise 3. Get 8 hours sleep tonight. Repeat. If you have trouble
falling asleep, consult your doctor.

Section Three: Amplify Your Creativity

- Once you've unlocked your natural creativity, it's time to grow it actively.
- To actively grow your creativity, double down on the two-step process of Modules 8 and 9: Feed story while suspending logic.
- Which you can do by leaning into the modules on the following pages.

Definitions

Perspective-Taking: A two-step process of (1) exiting your own perspective by seeing yourself from outside and (2) imagining the actions that another person would take.

Exceptional Information: Datapoints that do not fit established models, formulas, or expectations.

Reverse-Engineering: Speculating backward from causes to effects, from outcomes to actions, from events to actors.

Productive Conflict: A dispassionate collision of actions.

Module 13: Unplug Your Ego

The Zulus say that their great general Shaka was so devastated by the death of his mother Nandi that he ordered the slaying of every pregnant woman in Zululand. Now that he had lost his mother, there would be no more mothers across his empire.

This sounds like a myth. But it's true history, if not of Shaka then of our human psyche. That's because at the root of our psyche is an entity known as the ego. The ego thinks that the world exists for him. And from that core belief, the ego draws two logical deductions:

- What he thinks is true.
- What he feels is real.

The ego therefore concludes that when he is unhappy, the world must be unhappy as well. That's why the ego doesn't hesitate to throw temper tantrums, wallow in self-pity, and lash out with anger against anyone in his vicinity.

And the ego is also certain that he's always right. That's why he doesn't question his actions, no matter how much pain they cause. And that's why he never changes his mind, no matter how much havoc he creates. For if the ego were to admit that he was wrong, he would admit that there is something greater than him. Then the ego would shrink from being everything to being just another thing. Which to the ego, is death.

Ego isn't all bad, at least not from a scientific perspective. Ego helped keep your ancestors alive—and it can do the same for you. But as helpful as ego can be in certain situations, it's just one of your brain's many tools. So, you can shut it off (just like you can shut off logic) without harming yourself. And in fact, ego's temporary death can strengthen you. Without your ego, you'll boost your calm, your composure, your empathy, your introspection——and also, your creativity.

Your creativity is hampered by ego. Ego is proud and does not like to fail, but to be creative, you must stumble constantly. You must endure setbacks and even tragedies without sulking, withdrawing, or getting angry. And you must learn to accept that you're never completely right. Because even if you're right today, tomorrow will be different, and so tomorrow, you'll be wrong.

To be your most creative self, you must therefore learn humility. You must exit ego and look down on yourself with the greater eyes of life. You must learn to take a wry view of your failures—and more importantly, your successes—developing a healthy emotional detachment from all your behaviors.

When you do this, you'll sacrifice the pleasure of believing yourself to be the most important thing in the world. But you'll dramatically improve your potential for creative action. By stepping outside yourself, you'll learn to see your body as clay for your imagination to mold and your life as a story for your inspiration to script. When things go badly, you'll adapt. And when things go well, you won't get self-satisfied. You'll press your advantage by continuing to innovate.

The Zulus knew this. Which is why their tale ends with Shaka snapping out of his pout. Challenged by one of his subjects—a freethinking man by the name of Gala who says: *Are you so self-absorbed that you really think you're the first child to lose a mother?*—Shaka looks at himself with outside eyes, realizing how absurdly narcissistic he's being. And shaking free of his ego, he repeals his murderous decree—and returns to being one of the most innovative leaders in history.

You can do the same by adapting the Zulus' story into a simple neural trick: Imagine your own Gala. That is, imagine a person outside yourself who can serve as a mirror, reflecting your behavior back. See yourself in that mirror, looking at your behavior with outside eyes. And then adjust your actions from that external perspective, discovering how easy it is to change your behavior once you let go of your ego and take a broader view.

By doing this, you activate your brain's perspective-taking circuitry, allowing you to see through other eyes, expand your outlook, and be more than yourself. And once you've enriched your mind with one Gala, add more. Be like Shaka, who surrounded himself with a council of advisors, each with their own individual perspective. Think of all the wise people you know—and imagine what they would advise you to do. Cycle between their different perspectives, exploring how you can mold your body in all the different ways they recommend.

That range of motion is just the start of what you can achieve. Because once you exit your ego, you can do anything.

Exercise 1. Get yourself a workout manual and select a new exercise. Attempt the exercise with your eyes closed. Now open your eyes and attempt the same exercise in front of a mirror, observing your body with outside eyes. Note how much easier it is to train your body in an original movement when you feel like you're watching it from outside.

Exercise 2. Identify an activity or pursuit that you would like to do, but that makes you feel nervous or intimidated. Now, activate your brain's perspective-taking circuitry to step outside yourself. See your body as a tool to manipulate, a puppet to control, a body that isn't you. Then direct that body to do the activity or pursuit. Experience how much easier it is to command yourself from outside.

Exercise 3. Identify a creative project that you dropped because you felt it wasn't good enough. Return to that project and exit your ego. Tell yourself that it's someone else's project and your role is simply to make sure that it gets executed in a timely manner. Tell yourself it doesn't need to be perfect; just adequate. Because it isn't a reflection on you and your ego; it's just a job to be completed.

Exercise 4. Once you've finished the creative project in Exercise 3, think of a creative person you respect. Enter their perspective and look at the project. Then revise and edit parts of the project that, from your new outlook, you now see that you can improve.

Module 14: Seek the Exceptional

Saladin was always the exception to the rule.

Born a medieval Kurd, he became a hero of the modern Arab world. By faith a Sunni, he served Shiite caliph. The heir of humble village folk, he founded a dynasty that stretched across the Middle East and down the Nile. The champion of Islam, he sought peace with Christian Crusaders—until their broken truces propelled him to take Jerusalem with war. A conqueror of mythic riches, he was so generous to his subjects that at his death, his wallet did not hold enough copper coins to pay for his burial.

But perhaps Saladin's greatest exception was the book he carried. It was not a book he'd been given in school; there he'd been drilled in the logical formulas of geometry, astronomy, and the law. Nor was it his era's most universal text: the Quran. Instead, the book was a poetry anthology assembled by the renegade ninth-century poet Abu Tammam.

Tammam was a maverick advocate of innovation. Against the traditionalists of his age, who believed in an eternally perfect literary style, Tammam thought that poetry was withered by repetition—and kept alive by evolution. To inspire that imaginative growth in later generations, Tammam gathered together 881 of the most powerful Arabic poems in history. And he showed: those poems were all original. They had their own unique voice, their own individual creations. What made them powerful was thus not that they were universally timeless, but that they dared to do something new.

In recognition of this creative courage, Tammam's anthology became known as the *Ḥamāsa*—the *Bravery*. This was the book carried everywhere by Saladin, who imbibed its poetry so thoroughly that he eventually memorized it, quoting its thousands of verses by heart. And like the authors of those verses, Saladin discovered that the key to creativity was not to stick to eternal rules—but to courageously seek the exception.

This seeking of the exceptional is the secret to the adaptive intelligence of the human brain. The human brain learned, through millions of years of biological evolution, that the exception was the first sign of an emergent threat or opportunity. By fixating on those signs, the human brain trained itself to anticipate the future, so it was always prepared to cope with sudden dangers or exploit new advantages.

And so the human brain became the winner of the war for life. While other, rule-focused brains were surprised by disaster or too slow to seize their chance for triumph, the human brain leveraged outlying datapoints into groundbreaking tactics, staying one step ahead of the biological curve.

Yet even though this is how our species became the dominant life on earth, we're in danger of losing our inborn instinct for exceptional information. That's because, just like Saladin, we live in a world where we're all taught to prioritize the universal. In Saladin's day, that universal was medieval logic and theology. In our day, it's statistics, spreadsheets, metrics, computer AI, and other logic-based systems for crunching data into general rules of action. Those systems treat outlying datapoints as blips and aberrations to be smoothed out of the curve or regressed to the mean. They condition us to believe that the weird is a glitch, an aberration, a blip to be ignored.

And most of the time, they're right. Most of the time, the weird signal _is_ a random anomaly that means nothing. Most of the time, the smart thing to do is dismiss it.

But not always. Because some of those outliers are the first indication that the existing order is about to collapse. They're warnings of impending volatility. They're a heads-up that we have to adapt now—or risk extinction.

So, if you want to adapt in those moments of rapid instability when battles swing and history pivots, raising new empires and toppling the old, you will treat every outlier as potentially significant. You will pause and consider what the future would look like if that exception became the new rule. You will ask yourself: _What could this potentially mean? If this is possible, then what else is possible? What unprecedented future is hinted in this weird piece of evidence?_

Which is to say: You will not act like a computer. You will not smooth out strange new data to conform to familiar old rules. You will act like your human forerunners. You will reconnect with your brain's primal intuitions. You will actively respect rogue blips, treating them not as freak facts but as exceptional information.

With that exceptional information in hand, you'll be able to make fast conjectures about how events might be turning. And you'll then be able to test those conjectures, quickly, with light probes that don't commit you to radically changing your current strategy. Your probes will reveal if the blip is, as most blips are, a blip to be ignored. But your probes will also put you on the front foot if the blip is that inescapable war-event: the sudden shift that changes everything. Then you'll be able to meet the future while your adversaries lag.

That's the lesson of Saladin's book: don't prefer statistical reliability to world-changing epiphanies, when what you want is *both*. You want to acknowledge that the exceptional is unrepresentative—and therefore probably untrustworthy. But you also need to acknowledge that every new danger and every new advantage begins with an instant where an exception breaks logic, inviting untold disaster—or spectacular victory.

So, instead of filtering out the strange and the outlying, learn to tune it in. Be sensitive to peculiar details and be curious about where they lead, suspending judgment to speculate on unknown possibilities ahead. Because if you don't acquire the habit of active anticipation, then when exception really strikes—which it inevitably will—you'll be a fatal step behind, and surprise will be your ambush not your ally.

Exercise 1.   Write down every event today that strikes you as out of the norm. Follow up on each one and note whether it portended anything.

Exercise 2.   Draw up a list of people in your unit and note one thing that's unique about their perspective. Imagine

a situation where that unique perspective could solve
a problem or exploit an opportunity.

Module 15: Neutralize Your Hopes and Fears

On 5 November 1757, across a treeless, hilly patch of the Holy Roman Empire, the Battle of Rossbach began and ended in less than ninety minutes. But despite the battle's brief length, it made Frederick the Great famous forever.

At Rossbach, Frederick crushed an army twice his size, routing 40,000 French and Imperial flintlock musketeers in abject terror. His victory stunned Europe and in later years has been ascribed to many factors: disciplined and rapid-firing infantry; decisiveness at critical junctures; swiftly adaptive artillery; creative use of fast movement, flanking, and oblique order.

All these were tremendously significant. But they don't fully explain Frederick's stunning triumph. Because they'd all been part of his arsenal five months earlier at the Battle of Kolin, when he'd been humiliated under similar conditions. There was something new at Rossbach, something that hadn't existed at Kolin. And it was this: a new mindset in Frederick—and his army.

The shift had begun in the final, desperate moments at Kolin. There, Frederick's soldiers had cracked. Battered by cannon and shocked by bayonet, they'd started to abandon their positions and run. Appalled, Frederick had galloped to their waving ranks and screamed: *Hünde, wollt ihr euwig leben?—"You dogs! Do you really want to live forever?"*

The question would later become legend, summoned again and again as a rallying cry in frantic trenches and deadly beachheads. But at the time, it was utterly original, an invention so singular that it stunned Frederick's junior officers. Had their commander lost his mind? Why was he doing the opposite of what every other successful commander in history had done? Why wasn't he making his troops the usual promise that they would live forever, immortalized in Valhalla or some other warrior heaven? Why was he instead mocking eternity and snarling at his soldiers to run into death?

But to the amazement of Frederick's officers, Frederick's question worked. His panicked soldiers regained their courage. And although they could not turn the tide of that battle already lost, they did stabilize the retreat. Heroically covering the flight of their frightened colleagues, they prevented a massacre, ensuring that the army survived to fight again.

As amazing as this feat seemed at the time, modern neuroscience has discovered why Frederick's invention was so effective: it neutralized the brain's hopes and fears.

Hopes and fears are the most powerful drivers of human behavior. They originate in our brain's ancient core, the amygdala, from where they radiate outward, swaying the rest of our neuroanatomy. And of those potent emotions, the most potent are our fear of death—and our hope for immortal life. To a biological creature such as ourselves, life is everything and death the final ending. So, nothing stirs more raw panic or courage in our brain than the thought of perishing now or living forever.

Those strong emotions can be useful motivators in certain circumstances, but most of the time, they have the negative effect of limiting our adaptability. Swamping out our brain's creative circuits, they warp our mental narratives into projections of our personal dreams and anxieties. So, instead of freely imagining what *could* happen, we can only imagine what we wish would happen——or what we're afraid will happen. The universe of potential futures collapses into two narrow alternatives, cramping innovation and trapping us in our own private heavens and hells.

Frederick's question sprung his men from that trap. By prompting them to imagine that they were already dead, it liberated them to see a broader range of options for creative action. (Or, to be technical, it activated the perspective-taking regions of their prefrontal cortex, giving them a sense of mental distance from their egocentric emotions and enabling them to plan more flexibly.)

This mental shift made Frederick's soldiers calmer in the face of battle, and it also boosted their creativity, unchaining their brains to plot beyond the tight constraints of their nagging anxieties and wishful fantasies. The resulting increase in adaptive intelligence allowed them to innovate faster on the battlefield, dynamically neutralizing emergent threats and exploiting fresh opportunities.

This is why Frederick's artillery and infantry were so famously adaptive, rearranging themselves on the battlefield with apparently preternatural intelligence. They couldn't actually see the future, but they seemed like they could. By vacating their hopes and fears, they became swifter at reacting to changing circumstance, so that instead of being made by war's fast-evolving environment, they helped to make it.

To achieve a similar creative zen, ruthlessly destroy your own dreams and worries. Remind yourself: the best things in life are usually unexpected and most anxieties are irrational, self-centered concerns that never materialize. Practice ironic self-distancing, satirizing your personal apprehensions and ambitions. Place yourself in the position of a dispassionate observer, listening neutrally to others and to the world around you.

And above all, do what Frederick's soldiers did: make peace with the fact that you are nothing, that you died before this day began, that all that matters is the greater narrative beyond.

Exercise 1.   Write down the things you're most personally afraid of happening—and the things you most hope to happen. Tell yourself that they've already occurred and then get on with life.

Exercise 2.   Imagine that, right now, you're a ghost. You cannot die because you're already dead. You cannot go to hell or heaven because this place, here, is your eternal home. Your only purpose is to help the people here adapt to their changing future. What do you see in that future? What's your first advice for them?

Module 16: Get Environmentally Dynamic

In May 1945, Võ Nguyên Giáp met the Americans.

Giáp was the commander of Ho Chi Minh's communist insurgents, fighting to drive Japanese imperialists out of his home country of Vietnam. As a communist, he'd been trained to believe in ideology's eternal rules. Those rules were born of absolute reason and hence they always worked, in every situation—or so, at least, the party faithful believed.

But from the Americans, Giáp learned a different perspective. That perspective was what they called "active flexible response." Or in other words, adapting yourself to the situation. Active flexible response wasn't achieved by sticking to absolute rules. It was achieved by the opposite: creativity. And creativity was fed not by ideological uniformity but by dynamic tension.

That's why the American political system had two competing parties, not one unopposed communist faction. That's why the Americans prized diversity, individuality, freethinking, and other sources of social divergence. And that's why the Americans welcomed hard physical environments. Hard physical environments forced you to struggle against them. And that struggle helped foster the culture of innovation with which the America's founding heroes had defeated the British Empire. While the British had tried to impose their ordered redcoat formations onto the rugged colonial landscape, the Americans had embraced the material and mental hardships posed by thick woods and wild swamps, leveraging the terrain's resistance to human movement into inventive guerrilla tactics.

For the next thirty years, Giáp held onto this different perspective. He used it to drive out the Japanese by ambushing their outposts with American flamethrowers. A decade later, in the summer of 1954, he used it to tuck Soviet howitzers into the jungle hillsides around Dien Bien Phu, hammering back the French Army's colonial occupiers. And another decade later, in the mid-1960s, he used it to implement what US National Security Agency described as "one of the great achievements of military engineering of the 20th century." That great achievement was the Ho Chi Minh Trail.

The Ho Chi Minh Trail was an intricate maze of gravel roads, bicycle trails, and footpaths that stretched from the supply yards of North Vietnam to the battlefields of the South. It could move 30 tons of equipment a day, through even thigh-high, monsoon mud. And perhaps more importantly, it inculcated in Giáp's soldiers the same culture of adaptive strength that the guerilla tactics of 1776 had inculcated in America's original freedom-fighters, enabling Giáp's soldiers to do to the Americans what the Americans had earlier done to the British Empire: out-adapt, out-innovate, and outmaneuver them.

You can reap the same creative benefit from the environment. The environment is alien and unpredictable, which is why the average twenty-first-century American seeks to keep it at bay with air conditioning and digital playgrounds. But nature is not our enemy. Nature is the engine of life—and the source of creativity. The more we try to dominate or repress nature, the more fragile we make our own culture. But the more we embrace nature's volatile pushback, the more we feed off its creative energy to become creators ourselves.

And the same that goes for nature goes for any environment. In the strategic environment of war, embrace the adversity of uncertainty, feeling it feed your ingenuity. In the tactical environment of local combat, embrace the punch of your adversary, feeling it feed your fluidity. And in the social environment of others, embrace the resistance of their opinions. Don't bully your subordinates into silencing their objections; and don't duck the oversight of your superiors by cloaking your intentions. Onboard their oppositional perspectives, feeling them grow your imagination. The more of the outside world that you can internalize, the more you'll enhance your adaptive intelligence.

The more of nature's big struggle you admit into your life, the more you'll become like nature: resilient, dynamic, and boundlessly creative.

Exercise 1. Make a list of things you don't like about your current work situation or institutional environment.

Then embrace those negatives as positive challenges, leveraging their resistance into adaptive change.

Exercise 2. Invite the people around you to submit anonymous critiques of your current approach. Don't reject the critiques or change because of them. Instead, memorize them. Then recall the critiques during your next task or mission, allowing them to flow through your mind and seeing what new options for action they open.

Module 17: Invent Backward then Forwards

The most famously creative strategist in Western history is Odysseus. Sometime during the Bronze Age, likely in the twelfth-century BC, he contrived the ruse of the Trojan Horse, ending a bloody ten-year stalemate between the thousand ships of Greece and the armed citadel of Ilium.

But as a recently discovered African scroll has revealed, Odysseus adapted his ruse from someone else: the Egyptian general Djehuty. Two-and-a-half centuries before Odysseus, Djehuty tricked the inhabitants of the rebel city of Joppa into accepting a tribute of a hundred baskets. A tribute that was a trick: inside the baskets were a hundred Egyptian warriors who, once inside the city, leapt out and seized it for their pharaoh.

This earlier Egyptian trick might seem to diminish Odysseus's claim to being a creative genius. But the opposite is true. It proves that Odysseus had mastered one of creativity's most practical techniques: adapting an old innovation to a new use.

That process of adaptation is how life's most useful tools evolved. The human brain adapted the old innovation of the animal neuron into a new hub of ingenuity. And our body's most useful tool evolved in the same way: our opposable thumb is an adaptation of the older innovation of the mammalian paw.

The same holds true with most of the subsequent things that our brains and opposable thumbs have invented: they're clever re-tweaks of older gadgets. Which is why the most effective way to innovate isn't to forget all the existing technology on the shelf. If you do that, you'll usually just end up reinventing the wheel. Instead, the better route is to start with the wheel—and invent a *better* one.

To pull off that feat, start with a technology, a tactic, or some other innovation you admire. Then work backward from what the innovation does to _how_ it was invented. With this mental reverse, you shift your focus from _product_ to _process_, uncovering the deeper creative method that generated the invention. You can then redeploy that creative method to generate *more* innovations, so that instead of endlessly recycling yesterday's breakthroughs, you tap into the infinite possibility that produced them.

This is what Odysseus did when he reverse-engineered Djehuty's tactic, adapting Egyptian baskets into his Trojan Horse. And it's what Djehuty did too. Where, exactly, Djehuty got the idea for his basket subterfuge, we cannot say. But we can guess that the tale of the baskets is a poetic fiction adapted from an earlier historical truth: Djehuty served under Pharaoh Thutmose III, who with the help of his generals, captured much of the Near East, from the Euphrates to the fourth cataract of the Nile, becoming revered as Egypt's most successful conqueror.

Those conquests were achieved by adapting a series of technological innovations—such as the horse-drawn chariot and the sickle sword—that Thutmose inherited from earlier wars between the Egyptians and the invading Hyksos. Those innovations had, in their original form, won many a city. But when remixed and upgraded by Thutmose's military engineers, they won an astonishing 350 cities, transforming Egypt into the greatest empire of the early Bronze Age.

And that's the real key to the strategic genius of Djehuty and Odysseus. Not baskets, wooden horses, or other bits of fakery. But reverse-engineering an old technique or tactic to fit a new situation.

Exercise 1.   Identify an old protocol that you've used successfully. Research the protocol, learning the process of how it was created. Then apply that creative process to a new problem you're facing and see what solutions emerge.

Exercise 2.   Select a battle from history. Identify the crucial tactical decision that led to victory. Then isolate the deeper process—the deeper *why*—that led to that decision. And imagine a way to implement that *why* in a modern battle situation.

Module 18: Harness Conflict

Marathon. Thermopylae. Salamis.

They're the ancient world's most inspirational military trilogy. They prove that war is won not with brute power but with creative strategy. Three times, in wildly different circumstances, the Greeks deployed inventiveness to defeat Persia's million-man invasions, the mightiest in history.

How did the Greeks do it? What was the secret of their genius? How did they become such effective strategists?

The answer is: before the Greeks fought against the Persians, they fought against each other.

The fighting began in Sparta, which, by the sixth-century BC, had come to be ruled by two kings. Two kings. An impossible number. Two kings meant disagreement, tension, conflict. Surely, the two kings would split Sparta apart, until there were two Spartas, each with one king, the logical number.

But the two kings worked. Not that they didn't fight with each other. They did. Yet they were mightier than any of Greece's solo kings. And at the end of the sixth-century BC, they marched their armies east—and toppled the one king of Athens.

With that king gone, Sparta tried to make Athens a second Sparta, ruled by two kings. But the Athenians went further. Instead of two kings, they opted for thousands, making every Athenian citizen his own liege. This was democracy, and it was even more contentious than Sparta's two-ocracy. The citizens of Athens struggled endlessly with each other. And then they went to war with Sparta, so that the two cities became like two competing kings, battling for control of Greece.

This Greek state of constant inner conflict was not planned. But it was not entirely accidental, either. Back in the seventh-century BC, the celebrated Greek poet Hesiod had rhapsodized in *Works and Days* that the goddess Strife came in two shapes. The first was the source of civil war. The second, of civil prosperity:

For when a man sees that the man next door is wealthy,

He hastens to plow his fields and work his farm better.

Neighbor strives with neighbor, inspiring each to outdo

The other, making both wealthy. This is good Strife.

It pits potter against potter, carpenter against carpenter,

Beggar against beggar—and singer against singer.

This "good strife" is what Sparta institutionalized with its two kings. Those two kings competed for glory, forcing each other to work harder—not just physically, but mentally. Each had to wrack his brain for the cleverest plans and strategies. Each had to battle against complacency to be his more ingenious self.

That positive conflict was multiplied in Athens. To lead Athens successfully, you had to outwit more than one other mind. You had to outwit every other mind in the democracy. You had to be the winner of ten thousand mental battles. So, you trained your brain relentlessly. And you tested yourself constantly against your peers, waging intellectual combat in streets and in stadiums.

This is why the Greeks outwitted the Persians. The Persians were born as intelligent as the Greeks. And they benefited from an excellent military education. But that education was installed within a one-king system that limited disagreement. When the Persian generals differed, the king made the final decision. And so the generals learned that the path to success was always the same: please the king. This warped the entire political system around the preferences of a lone individual. Instead of multiplying creative intelligence, it focused the Persians on obedience and flattery, narrowing their strategy and making it brittle.

And this is why the Greek model became the basis of later governments that shocked the world with unthinkable victories. First, there was Rome, which adapted Sparta's two kings into its two republican consuls, creating a culture of perpetual self-struggle that launched a nobody Italian tribe into conquering Carthage, Greece, and Egypt. Then there were the 13 American colonies, who consciously incorporated both the Roman and the Greek systems into their own founding documents, promoting an inner contest of leadership at the 1774 Continental Congress that almost tore apart the fledging United States—before knocking back the British Empire.

This embrace of good strife is risky. It promotes infighting and can easily lead to civil war, as both Rome and America discovered. But it's a guaranteed source of creativity because it harnesses the same root process of conflict that drives biological evolution in nature.

The key to maximizing its productive yield is to get as much of the good strife (creativity) without the bad (civil war). Which you can do by. . .

(1) Enriching your mind with competing viewpoints, nurturing conflict within yourself. No matter how divided your mind gets, your left brain will never literally invade your right, so you can aggressively seek to be of two (or more minds) without risking actual physical destruction.

(2) Building strong emotional bonds with the people in your creative team. Those bonds are the foundation of healthy strife. The more you trust and care about each other, the more comfortable you'll be disagreeing—and the more productively you'll compete. You'll sharpen each other's plans and plots with honest pushback, and share the proud feeling of accomplishment when a rival strategy wins.

(3) Establishing a shared narrative. By finding common cause, you can set aside petty ego and harness difference for gain. The common cause of freedom is what unified the Athenians and the Spartans against the Persians. And if the Athenians and Spartans—who fought endless, bloody wars against each other—could find a shared narrative, so can anyone.

No military has ever reached its potential by promoting a top-down culture of consensus. Which is why even the most totalitarian regimes discover that they must admit some peer-to-peer competition to achieve strategic greatness. What would the WW2 Soviet Army have achieved without the constant disagreements of Konstantin Rokossovsky and Georgy Zhukov?

To commit fully to this path you must once again shut off logic. Logic teaches that conflict is a waste of energy. So, logic does its best to eliminate conflict by using metrics, data, spreadsheets, and rational analysis to identify the better answer or the harmonious synthesis. Which is to say: logic promotes a one-king system. That's why rationalists from Plato onward have insisted that monarchy is superior to democracy. Better to have a philosopher-king than a squabbling mob.

We learn the opposite from plotting. Every good plot begins with a conflict. It's conflict between characters, or conflict between characters and their world, that drives creative storylines ahead.

So, to increase creativity, stow your inner logician and activate your neural plotting. Don't dampen conflict; commit to both sides of every mental struggle and encourage them evenly. See conflict as a generative force not a destructive one, and don't be afraid to stoke it. To ensure the stoking is as productive as possible, divorce conflict from fears, hopes, and other things of ego. Make it a conflict of dispassionate actions, each of which is necessary and neither of which can be compromised.

Because the longer you can remain—as an individual or as an organization—in a state of healthy inner tension, the more likely you are to hatch a winning innovation.

Exercise 1. Identify an action that you're of two minds about. Then commit yourself fully to doing both the action and its opposite, pressing on the conflict until creative solutions materialize.

Exercise 2. Identify a person in your life who holds a perspective that you think is wrong. Suspend your objections and ask <u>the</u> person to explain <u>why</u> they hold that perspective. Identify how their <u>why</u> differs from your <u>why</u>. Then tackle a creative problem with the two different <u>whys</u> in mind, not resting until you've identified a solution that satisfies both.

Section Four: Practice, Practice, Practice

- Creativity is a muscle; the more you exercise it, the more it'll be there when needed.

- Now that you've located your core creative muscles, bulk them up through repetition.

- Here are some workouts that will give back whatever you give.

Module 19: Twister

Creative strategy is born from the unprecedented. The unprecedented provides the *need* for adaptive intelligence and so the *opportunity* for creative strategizing.

  The successful strategist will therefore anticipate the unprecedented, transforming himself to match its shifting landscape. To achieve this oneness with situational flux, the creative strategist must learn to anticipate life's turning points. Doing this can seem to require mystic intuition. But neuroscience has regularized it into a two-step procedure:

  (1) Survey each environment for its unique laws of action, that is, the laws that govern what can happen and what cannot.

  (2) Employ your brain's planning muscles to hypothesize unprecedented consequences of those laws, plotting out what *could* happen but hasn't yet.

This procedure is known as plot-twisting, and the more you practice it, the more you'll learn to see plot twists as routine occurrences. So, even if you don't identify life's specific twists, you'll embrace them more confidently and leverage them faster, thriving in uncertainty and out-adapting your competitors.

Exercise 1. Identify a conflict within your workspace or organization. The conflict can be healthy or unhealthy; that is, it can promote unit function or degrade it. Trace the conflict back to a common assumption that the people in that space have about appropriate behavior. That assumption is an environmental rule of action. Now, imagine three unprecedented consequences of the rule. Trace how each changes the conflict.

Exercise 2. Revisit a historical battle. What special law of action was imposed on that battle by the terrain, the weather, the technology, the culture, the personalities at play? After identifying the law, imagine three unexpected consequences that it could have had in the battle.

Exercise 3. Identify a future theater of war or other zone of potential hostile conflict. Isolate one rule of operation that makes that theater unique. What are three unprecedented outcomes that could result from that rule?

Module 20: Predictor

Conflict situations don't afford the luxury of time. Events escalate fast, and you can't pause the action to speculate on every twist and turn that might arise.

To prepare for conflict, you therefore have to practice anticipating quicker—and you also have to practice *forgetting* faster, too. Because the longer you hang onto a prediction that doesn't pan out, the more it keeps you from being open to what's actually unfurling in front of you.

To build up this anticipating-forgetting capacity, start by getting yourself a plot-twisty book (like a thriller, a mystery, or a page-turning memoir). Then read the book a paragraph at a time, pausing briefly at the end of each paragraph to predict what happens in the next one.

When you move onto the next paragraph, compare your prediction to what actually happened, and then at the end of the next paragraph, repeat again. Continue this exercise until you can predict without pausing, then put aside your written narrative to practice on real-time ones. To start, try predicting the events of plot-twisty films, tv shows, and documentaries.

As you do this, *do not focus on whether or not you are predicting "correctly."* The more you fixate on getting your predictions right, congratulating yourself for accurate predictions and critiquing yourself for failed ones, the more you inhibit the development of your own creative flexibility. What matters more than anticipating correctly is anticipating *constantly*, so that you drill your brain in being fluid.

If your anticipations happen to be correct, that's great, but what shortens your reaction time isn't the occasional lucky strike; it's the learned habit of being narratively adaptable. And that habit is developed by setting aside your ego (which wants to be right about its predictions) and accelerating your rate of prediction—which you do by tightening the time horizon, focusing on near-term predictions that can be tested quickly with feedback and then just as quickly discarded.

Exercise 1.   Request to observe a meeting that involves personnel
               whom you don't know. Watch the meeting for a few
               minutes and then start to make active predictions
               about who will speak next and what they will say.
               Remember to actively forget each prediction before
               you move onto the next one. The long-term scorecard
               of your successes and failures will be retained by
               your brain's deep memory; if you hold it in your
               near-term consciousness, it will inhibit your
               creative openness.

Exercise 2.   Attend a sporting event. Pick one of the players and
               spend a few minutes getting into the flow of their
               actions. Then transition into actively predicting
               what they will do next. Repeat the same exercise
               with another player or two. See if you can predict
               not only what those players will do—but how they
               will interact or work together.

Module 21: Tweaker

The best strategies are the ones that are already ready-to-go; they're automatic to execute and inspire immediate confidence that builds when they unfold as practiced.

But how can creative strategies be ready-to-go? Don't they have to be constructed on the fly, in response to dynamic circumstance? Yes—but also no. Creative strategies need to be new, but they don't need to be *entirely* new. They just need to be new enough to meet the moment's unique opportunity, and often, that meeting can be created by a deft tweak to an existing strategy.

Which is to say: in practice, the most effective strategist is often not the one who makes up a revolutionarily original maneuver from scratch. It's often the strategist who takes a familiar old maneuver and gives it *just the right minor adjustment* to make it a perfect fit for the new situation presented.

To develop this skill, don't do the typical academic thing of playing Monday Morning quarterback, going back to lost battles with after-the-fact information to make better strategic decisions. All that does is strengthen your logic muscles.

Instead, go back to a <u>won</u> battle *and add a new obstacle*. Imagine what would happen if, at the moment that a winning strategy was deployed, the adversary countered it perfectly. How could the winning strategy be saved? How could it be tweaked to counter the counter? How could it be adjusted on the fly to resurrect its innovative action?

Exercise 1. Return in your mind to a success that you or your unit had. Imagine a plausible hitch you could have encountered but didn't. How could you counter that hitch to preserve your success?

Exercise 2. Study a historical battle where a weaker army defeated a stronger army through a superior tactic. Now imagine that the stronger army possessed that same tactic. Play the part of the weaker army and imagine a new

spin you can put on the tactic to outmaneuver the
stronger army and reclaim victory.

Module 22: Impersonator

Your brain can contain many brains.

That's because your brain has the power of perspective-taking. With that power, your brain can exit itself and examine its actions with an outside eye. And with that power, your brain can enter the minds of other people and plot like them.

This is what your brain does every time you read a memoir or watch a movie. It enters the minds of the characters and plans from their perspective, anticipating their actions.

And after you've finished reading or watching, your brain can carry those characters' minds with it. Your brain can think: *What would he do now? How would she respond to this situation that I'm in?*

The more you build up your brain's inner library of characters, the more dynamically adaptable it will become. Because instead of just relying on its own perspective, it can pull on the perspective of dozens, even hundreds, of other minds.

The first key to building that inner library is to make the characters in it psychologically diverse. So, read and watch widely. Don't confine your brain to people who remind you of yourself. Stretch to enter the minds of people who are creative in different ways.

The second key to building that library is to make it fast to access. So, don't memorize all the different choices and actions of another mind. Instead, identify the root _why_ that links together the mind's decisions and behaviors. To identify that _why_, ask yourself: What makes this particular mind special? What makes its perspective unique? What distinguishes it from other smart minds? What unusual things does it look for, emphasize, prioritize? What conventional things does it downplay? What original methods of planning and plotting does it employ?

Once you've built your inner library, the key to using it effectively is to practice rotating between your different inner characters—until, at the moment that action is necessary, you activate your "exit" perspective to make a dispassionate, fast decision.

That way, you feed your imagination with many perspectives. And then maximize your odds of practical success by taking the wider view.

Exercise 1.   Play a game against a friend. Don't try to beat him. Instead, try to <u>be</u> him. Make the decisions and play the moves that you think that he would make. The better you enter his head, the more you'll drive the game into stalemate. If you lose the game—or win—you're not there yet. Try again.

Exercise 2.   Identify a work problem that requires creativity to solve. Identify three people who you think would offer viable solutions. Enter their heads and provide an answer from each of their perspectives. Then step entirely back, using your brain's perspective-taking circuits to elevate you to what feels like a god's-eye view of the situation. And combine the three answers into your final course of action.

Module 23: Blender

What if Rommel fought Takeda Shingen at Gettysburg? What if Khalid Ibn al-Walid opposed the Duke of Wellington at the Battle of Moscow? What if Robert E. Lee and Genghis Kahn faced off at Agincourt?

With the skills you've built in the previous modules, you can now run all those simulations—and endless more. So go run them. Impersonate different adaptive intelligences fighting on foreign battlefields by mix-and-matching past strategists and situations.

To maximize the growth of your creative muscles, don't run the simulation to see who wins—instead, see how long you can keep the simulation going. Each time one side gets the upper hand, innovate the other's strategy.

That way, the only way for you to win is to sustain the conflict indefinitely.

Exercise 1.   Select a historical battle. Have the two opposing commanders switch sides. What happens next?

Exercise 2.   Select a historical battle. Now replace the losing general with a general from a different time and place. What does the new general do? How does the battle play out?

Exercise 3.   Select a historical military campaign. Then replace both commanders with commanders from different times and places. Have John Monash lead the Roman legions against Patton during the invasion of Gaul. Have Gustavus Adolphus command the Army of the Potomac against Louis Botha. How long can you keep the struggle balanced?

Module 24: Gamer

Operationalize the training you've developed over the previous modules by adding the dynamic elements of real-time speed, outside minds, and a changing environment (as in Module 20).

You can gain these elements by combining the previous modules into a wargame against a live human opponent. Avoid playing traditional computer or board games. Those games introduce the experience of playing against a dynamic adversary, but their weakness is that they institute an entirely stable environment, creating a decision space that an AI logician could master in advance.

Instead, opt for a *Kriegsspiel* with a situational domain that can be created, fresh, by the umpire at the start of every game (as in Module 23). Then enrich the *Kriegsspiel* with two additions:

(1) Empower the umpire to introduce unexpected plot twists (as in Module 19), forcing the players to adjust (as in Module 21).

(2) Empower the umpire to have the players switch sides (once or on multiple occasions), prompting each to adopt the strategic perspective of the other (as in Module 22).

A simplified version of this game can be played between two players:

1) Select a current military conflict.

2) Write the names of 20 different historical strategists on pieces of paper that are randomly shuffled in a bag.

3) Have one player imagine a plot-twist that could occur in the conflict (as in Module 19).

4) Have the other player draw a name from the bag—and respond to the twist from that strategist's perspective.

5) Swap roles and repeat until the bag is empty.

6) Put the names back in the bag and repeat with a different conflict.

Section Five: Advanced Creativity

- Now that you've trained your brain in creativity's basics, you can advance in three directions.

- One, you can learn to integrate creativity with logic, so that instead of segregating the two forms of intelligence, you partner them.

- Two, you can learn to leverage creativity into innovation, so that instead of just having more imaginative ideas, you have more imaginative ideas that _work_, amplifying your adaptive success.

- Three, you can learn to upscale creative thinking, getting more inventive ideas per minute.

Module 25: Failsafe Planning
(or, Partnering Logic with Creativity)

Most commanders are victims of their own personality.

Commanders who are bold by nature thrive in situations that call for boldness but struggle in situations that call for caution. Commanders who are by nature cautious do the opposite.

This is why Machiavelli claims that most military victories are really just luck. The winning commander chances into a battle that calls for his particular mental strength—and will be defeated as soon as he fights a battle that calls for a different strength.

And this is why Abraham Lincoln, Winston Churchill, and many other successful wartime leaders have cycled commanders when things bog down or a battle is lost. They assume that commanders cannot adapt, that they are what they are, that a bold leader cannot tread carefully and a cautious leader cannot bull the initiative.

And in most cases, this is true. It's very hard, as modern psychology has shown, for an instinctively aggressive personality to slow down or an instinctively thoughtful personality to speed up. And making it harder is that the brains of most successful commanders suffer from a survivorship bias: they've been promoted to their current role because their personality made them successful in their previous role. So, they're conditioned by experience to trust their gut instincts, making them inflexible.

But even though it's hard for commanders to evolve their core psychology, it's possible. George Washington managed it; so did Dwight Eisenhower. The key is humility, or to be more technical, self-distancing. Self-distancing, as we learned back in Modules 13 and 15, comes from exiting ego and neutralizing personal hopes and fears. It allows your brain to interrupt its habituated mental scripts and shift its perspective onto different action plans.

Self-distancing is nurtured by creativity. Which is why creative commanders can be bold but also cautious, adapting their strategy to what the situation requires. And it's also why creative commanders can learn _to shut their creativity off_.

Creativity, just like boldness and caution, is a virtue in some circumstances but a detriment in others. Specifically, creativity is a detriment in any situation that calls for compliance. You don't want to get creative when handling a firearm, running through a preflight check, or doing one of a million other tasks where the existing rules are working. That would waste time and endanger lives. It would unnecessarily bleed your operational capacity while allowing your adversary to build up strength. You only want to get creative when it's to your advantage to risk an experiment, when sticking to logic is actively diminishing your odds of success.

But how do you know when it's to your advantage to take that creative risk? How do you know when it's the smart thing to venture a new tactic—and when it's smarter to hang tight with procedure and trust the existing playbook?

The short answer is: it's hard to know for sure. Which is why many commanders get stuck in the personality trap. Just as commanders who are naturally bold tend to default to boldness, so do commanders who are naturally creative tend to default to creativity. And just as commanders who have previously succeeded by being cautious tend to default to caution, so do commanders who have previously succeeded by being logical tend to default to logic. So, instead of making the smart choice, they become victims of luck.

You can break out of that trap by exiting your personality and disciplining your brain to identify the difference between situations that call for logic—and situations that call for creativity.

Logic is effective in stable, certain environments. Creativity is effective in unstable, uncertain environments. To know when to toggle on/off creativity, the key is therefore to identify moments where an environment starts to transition from one state to the other.

Those transitions are typically rooted in the rise and fall of asymmetric conflict. As asymmetric conflict <u>increases</u>, stability erodes and uncertainty spikes, spawning the fog of war. As asymmetric conflict <u>recedes</u>, the reverse holds: a new stability emerges and the future becomes more reliably predictable.

When you notice either indicator, adjust your thinking in one direction or the other. And to keep you on the front foot, keep an eye out for the onset of asymmetric conflict. Since asymmetric conflict is the primary driver of situational chaos, be sensitive to any uptick in its range or intensity. The sooner an uptick is detected, the faster it can be de-escalated with a creative solution.

By learning to read these signs in your environment, you can maximize the benefits of both logic and creativity. Allowing you to adapt successfully to whatever life demands.

Exercise 1.   Do a personality self-inventory. Are you more instinctively inclined to be creative or logical? To remove that bias, distance yourself mentally from the bias's associated hopes and fears (e.g. "I am afraid that by being creative I will be too smart by half, creating unnecessary friction"; "I am afraid that by being logical I will be outflanked by a more agile adversary").

Exercise 2.   Identify areas of conflict in your environment and isolate the factors that make them—actually or potentially—asymmetric. Use that knowledge to determine whether you react to emergent problems with logic or with creative thinking.

Module 26: Honing Creativity into Innovation (Part I)

Creativity is pointless without innovation.

Innovation is creativity that works. Innovation is the practical purpose and entire object of creativity. Creativity for its own sake is idle play, or worse, vanity. Neither of which advances the mission.

So, if we could have innovation without creativity, we would. We would skip over the uncertainty and the inefficiency and jump right to the breakthrough.

But unfortunately, we can't. There's no way of knowing in advance whether something new will work. The new is, by its very nature, uncertain. That's what makes it different from logic's tried-and-true rules. That's why it should be ventured only when those rules aren't working. That's why every innovation in history has always come at the cost of some creative failure.

That's the bad news. Here's the good: there's a way to minimize the failure. The secret is *to aggressively seek the failure.*

Sounds counterintuitive. But it works for two simple reasons.

The first reason is psychological. By seeking creative failure, you rid yourself of the problem of overinvesting, emotionally and financially, in a creative idea succeeding. That overinvestment is the major source of boondoggles and other fanciful disasters. Our imagination is captured by the cleverness of a creative idea—and by all the wonderful things that would happen if the idea worked. So we focus on making the idea work, pouring time and money into troubleshooting an endlessly buggy project, when it would be more efficient to junk the idea and go with another.

The better psychological approach is to expect the idea to fail from the get-go. That expectation prevents you from falling in love with any one moment of creative inspiration. That expectation propels you into quickly testing the idea before you invest too much in its development, giving you rapid, objective feedback on its performance. And that expectation puts your confidence where it belongs: not in the creative product but the creative _process_. It's the creative process that is reliable, because the process enables you to generate a constant stream of potential ideas, ensuring that, eventually, you'll find one that works. Getting mentally wedded to a single idea is thus doubly counterproductive: it not only invites failure this time around, but separates you from the process required for future creative successes.

The second reason to aggressively seek failure is methodological. By seeking failure, you imagine: _What would it look like for this idea to crash? How could I make that crash happen as quickly as possible?_ That leads you to design tests that aggressively push the idea to its operational limit, quickly establishing the parameters under which the idea can function.

If those parameters are well below the needed threshold, then you can discard the idea quickly and painlessly. If those parameters are in range of the threshold, then you can pilot a few rapid solutions (expecting them, too, to fail) to see if you can boost performance. If those parameters meet or exceed the threshold, then you can count yourself pleasantly surprised. The idea proved itself, against your expectations, increasing the likelihood that it's a genuine innovation.

Put together, this methodology and psychology add up to a fast, experimental approach. They press you to imagine hard tests that you can perform now to yield quick feedback—and to push ideas dispassionately through those tests.

The result is to transition creativity as rapidly as possible into innovation. So, you neutralize creativity's shortcomings—unpredictability, inefficiency, fancifulness—while doubling-down on its strengths: flexibility, originality, bravery.

Exercise 1.   Identify a problem that calls for a creative solution. Write down the first solution that springs to mind. Then tell yourself mentally: _This solution has failed._ Now, write down the next solution that springs to mind. Repeat until you feel your confidence shifting from your individual ideas onto the overall process.

Exercise 2. Return to the answers you generated in Exercise 1. What's the cheapest, fastest way you could test each of them?

Module 27: Honing Creativity into Innovation (Part II)

At the end of the fifteenth century, Leonardo da Vinci invented the helicopter.

There was just one problem: the helicopter didn't fly. It couldn't generate enough upward thrust to elevate its power train. It spun forever on the ground, going nowhere.

But then, on 14 September 1939—more than 450 years later—the helicopter rose off the tarmac. What allowed it to fly was another invention, the combustion engine, plus some clever tweaks from Russian-American engineer Igor Sikorsky.

The lesson here is that creative ideas can fail, and fail, and fail, and fail before they succeed. So, how do you know, for sure, whether an idea won't work? How do you implement the training of the previous module—fast-test a prototype—without discarding an innovation worth of da Vinci? How can you decide whether you should move on when your invention doesn't fly—or whether you should attempt a Sikorsky?

The answer is that you cannot know for certain, because any idea can be made to work. That's the magic of creativity. Creativity can always invent fixes. With infinite time and infinite resources, Sikorsky's creativity could have made a battleship fly.

But unless you have infinite time and infinite resources, you don't want to chase that blue-sky possibility. You want to marshal the time and the resources you have to maximize the current odds of success.

Here's how you do that: you fast-test *multiple ideas* at once.

By fast-testing multiple ideas, you sketch the terrain in reach of capture, identifying what you can plausibly accomplish. That's because the ideas will all *succeed* in *different* ways, outlining the full range of what is possible. And the ideas will also all *fail* in the *same* ways, demarking the probable limits of progress in the here and now.

The payoff from fast-testing multiple ideas is thus different successes and identical failures, the first of which identifies what _can_ be accomplished, the second of which identifies what _cannot_. And when put together, the _can_ and the _cannot_ reveal what is feasible, here and now.

Fast-testing multiples thus guards against bias and inflated expectations. By revealing the varying potential of different ideas, it stops you from favoring any individual idea. And by revealing what failures are within acceptable limits, it protects you from too-hastily rejecting an idea that doesn't work perfectly. So, if the helicopter is a viable possibility, then fast-testing multiples will indicate that. But fast-testing multiples will also help you identify when the helicopter requires 450 years of further research, making it a poor investment now.

You can fast-test multiple ideas sequentially or simultaneously, so long as you test them all with equal vigor and don't prejudge any before the full round of testing is over.

But for fast-testing multiples to work, you must ensure that the ideas _are all fundamentally different_. If they're not fundamentally different, if they're all variants of the same core plan or design, then you're not really testing a range of ideas. You're simply testing the same idea, with three tweaks. That kind of testing is valuable, down the road, once you've identified your go-to candidate. But if you do it at the outset, you'll stymie innovation and invite drag and inefficiency.

If you've got too many ideas, and not enough time or resources to test them all, prioritize the ideas that are fastest and cheapest to test. This might feel counterintuitive. Shouldn't you instead test the ideas that inspire the most confidence in you?

No. That confidence is bias. All creative idea are potentially equal. There is _no_ _way_ to predict creative success—prediction is possible only in logical domains not creative one. So, from the perspective of innovation, the best idea is the idea that can be tested quickest. It provides the most bang for the buck.

And once you identify a winner, remember: you can always keep the other ideas around, in your memory. You don't have to delete them from history because they didn't work this time. Perhaps in a future situation, when you have different resources available, or shifted operational parameters, an idea that failed now will work.

That way, you can aggressively pursue whatever idea works quickest without worrying that you're giving up on a helicopter. If an idea can fly, it will eventually find its time.

Exercise 1.   Return to the list you generated in Module 26, Exercise 2. Circle the idea that's cheapest and fastest to test. That's your best idea. So, go test it. If it surprises you and works, it wins. If it fails as expected, delete it from your list and move rapidly on to your new best idea.

Exercise 2.   Identify three prototypes that have recently been devised to solve a similar technical problem, e.g., combat rifle, troop transport vehicle, long-range bomber. Or, identify three tactics that have been recently devised to exploit a similar battlefield situation. Mark the limits shared by all three prototypes (or tactics) and then identify the unique strengths of each of the prototypes (or tactics). Summed together, those common limits and individual strengths are your in-reach horizon.

Module 28: High Performance Creativity

Creativity reaches peak performance under just the right amount of pressure.

In high-pressure environments, your creative engine struggles to start. That's because high pressure triggers adrenaline, prompting your brain's fight-or-flight network, which in turn shuts down creativity. Your fight-or-flight network wants to act <u>now</u>. So, it either greenlights an existing strategy or hastily orders a retreat.

But high pressure isn't always bad for creativity. Quite the opposite: once your creative engine has started, it requires pressure to keep it humming. Without that pressure, your brain will conclude that there's no need to waste energy on further creativity; everything is copacetic, so it can just chill out on autopilot.

To maximize your brain's creative output, you therefore have to initiate it at low pressure and feed it with increasing pressure, like an engine you ignite with a small burst of gas before opening the throttle.

Outside of life-and-death situations, the most challenging part of this operation is the throttle. You must elevate the urgency artificially, via imposed deadlines or forced competition.

In life-and-death situations, the challenge is the opposite. You must mentally escape the pressure of your situation, before gradually reintroducing it. This is why effective commanders can often seem eerily detached or cheerfully tranquil under fire; they have learned to dissociate from their immediate reality to allow their brain to draw on its full creative resources, without lapsing into short-term fight-or-flight. And it's also why those same commanders can transition suddenly into adrenaline speed, fueling their strategic imagination once they've got it kickstarted.

The only way to develop this ability is through practice. The ability to start calm and then switch on the intensity is not inborn. It does not magically happen to people when they arrive in their first warzone. If people have a natural tendency to dissociate in moments of stress, they will stick in the ignition part of the process, never proceeding to the throttle. If people are naturally high-strung, they will flood their creative engine, never getting it to fire.

So, to maximize your adaptive intelligence, practice managing pressure. Put yourself in situations with elevated stakes—and then train yourself to dissociate from your environment, consciously relaxing your mind to create a protected inner space where your creativity can engage. Once you feel your creativity working, gradually let in the stress of your situation, powering your ingenuity with feedback and dynamic constraint.

That's your high-performance mind. That's your pistons firing at their fastest.

Exercise 1.   Identify an unpredictable environment, natural or artificial. Enter it and practice dissociating by telling yourself:

> *This is not happening to me. . .I am not here. . . this is not real, it's just something I'm watching on a television screen.*

Once you're dissociated, begin focusing on the actions around you, one at a time, maintaining your feeling of distance but elevating your creative engagement.

Exercise 2.   Identify a problem that you know that one of your superiors wants solved. Devote an hour of free time to casually brainstorming potential solutions. Then tell your superior that you have a completed answer that you will present next week. Use the adrenaline of that imposed deadline to accelerate the brainstorm you initiated in a relaxed environment.

Module 29: Break Inertia

Inertia is inevitable.

Not because the human brain is naturally lazy. The human brain is in fact naturally restless. That's why the world is full of anxiety and edgy boredom. That's why so many people use nicotine, alcohol, and other chemicals to forcibly relax.

No, inertia is inevitable because of a paradox that arises within physical environments. The paradox is that the environment's inhabitants are more aware than outsiders of its problems. But they're also more close-minded about potential solutions. So, they're more conscious of the need for innovation but also less willing to try new things.

This is why workers grumble about their jobs but are also pessimistic—even fatalistic—about change. This is why soldiers know exactly what's wrong with their unit, but steel themselves to accepting the same-old troubles without complaint.

This paradox emerges for a simple reason: the longer we spend time in an environment, the more things we've seen fail or go wrong. That experience thus makes us an expert on what needs to change. But also cynical that improvement is possible.

The result is a drag on innovation. Instead of actively improving, units stagnate until a crisis triggers a panicked reaction, which typically leads less to thoughtful progress than to overreaction.

Breaking this culture is psychologically difficult. But practically straightforward. The best way is through unit crosspollination. To achieve that crosspollination:

(1) Partner two units.

(2) Have each unit draw up a list of its problems.

(3) Have each unit propose creative solutions to the other unit's problems.

This method has three practical gains:

(1) It provides each unit with a list of potentially useful solutions, generated by independent, outside eyes.

(2) It combats cynicism by demonstrating to each unit that they can come up with creative solutions to another unit's difficulties. This capacity to be helpful to others has been scientifically demonstrated to boost our optimism and resilience when troubleshooting our own problems.

(3) It energizes further creative thinking by activating each unit's pride. No one wants to be told by outsiders how to fix their personal business. No one wants to admit they aren't masters of their own domain. So, the process stimulates each unit to prove that they can come up with better solutions to their problems themselves.

This same process can also be used by individuals. Find someone whom you respect—and whom you also want to respect you. Tell him your problems. Then ask him how to fix your life. You'll get some good ideas. And more importantly, you'll be lightly chagrined into coming up with better ideas yourself—and to then implement those ideas, proving that they work.

This is the biological reason that pride exists in the brain. Not to make us self-satisfied. But to combat the fatalism that breeds stasis.

Exercise 1. Make a list of three problems in your life that you want fixed, but feel are unfixable. Then identify a peer whom you want to impress, or even see as a rival. Have the courage to show them your list of problems and ask for advice. Appreciate their recommendations—but tell yourself that you can do even better.

Exercise 2. Identify a unit that you regard as a competitor. Ask for their advice with an internal problem—and use that advice to motivate you to out-compete the other unit.

Module 30: Scale Creativity

Now that you've reached the end of this book, your creative engine is humming. You've tuned the sparkplugs, timed the belts, revved the horsepower, and maxed out the torque.

But even if you're squeezing every last bit of performance from your onboard mental pistons, you can still increase your creativity. That's because creativity isn't confined to individual brains. It can be a group activity. Just as you can increase a computer's logical processing by networking it with another computer, so too can you increase a human brain's creative thinking by linking it to other brains.

You've experienced this basic phenomenon when you've brainstormed in teams. You've discovered that a team can come up with ideas that no individual member could have imagined alone. You've discovered that human creativity can *scale*.

You can get this power-boost simply by putting two people in a room with a shared problem. Their brains will naturally partner, generating a creative thinker that's more than the sum of its parts. This is because humans evolved as social animals. So, our brains evolved to function in tandem. Without the need for any special instruction, our brains know, by instinct, how to combine.

But even so, science has revealed that this natural process of brain-combination can be optimized. The key is a group version of the high-performance protocol we covered in Module 28. The group version has two stages:

(1) **Ignition.** In this phase, reduce stress and build trust, kickstarting creativity by adopting an anything-goes "Yes, And" method. That method works just the way it sounds. Whenever someone has an idea, don't say "No, But." Say "Yes, And," validating the new idea while simultaneously extending it, building positive energy and momentum.

(2) **Throttle.** In this phase, transition from open creativity onto load-bearing. First, have the group pool its experience to identify potential hitches—and propose tweaks and solutions. Then harness the group to develop

quick tests (as in Module 27), shifting from free creativity into innovation.

The bigger the group, the more creative potential it has—but the harder it is to achieve ignition. So for fastest results, start with a small team of three or four members, then feed in new creatives once the super-engine is humming.

Exercise 1. Invite two members of your unit to solve a problem with you. Eliminate pressure initially by presenting it as a side project. Then once you've got the ideas flowing, ramp up the pressure by proposing that the team present its conclusions at a bigger meeting, next week.

Exercise 2. Return with your group to one of the problems you identified in Module 27. See how the group solves it differently than you did, solo.

Conclusion: Ten Myths About Creativity

Myth One: Creativity Comes from Genius

You can thank Clausewitz for this myth. He got everything else right, but not this. Creativity doesn't come from some mysterious, supernatural essence. It's a scientific process, built into the structure of the animal neuron, rooted in the same physical mechanism that drives evolution by natural selection. Which is why you can methodically practice creativity and see consistent, practical gains.

Myth Two: Some Original Ideas Are Obviously Better Than Others

All original ideas are created equal. There's no way to guess which ones will work until they're put to an empirical test. That's why ideas that seem weird or impossible can surprise everyone, starting a revolution. If you're absolutely sure that an original idea will (or won't work), then you're lapsing into bias. (Or, the idea isn't really original.)

Myth Three: Creative People Are Flighty and/or Emotional

Creativity is a form of intelligence. So, it's as rigorous as logic, just in a different way. The most successfully creative people are therefore highly disciplined. And while creativity can be boosted by certain forms of emotion—specifically, optimism, empathy, and curiosity—creativity is scattered by fear, desire, and other egoistic passions.

Myth Four: Creative People Are Born That Way

It's true that some people are born with psychological traits——such as openness—that can enhance creativity. But the primary source of creativity is the _desire_ to be creative. That desire comes more naturally to some people than others, but it can be cultivated in anyone. With that desire, you can do what Caesar, Shakespeare, and the world's other greatest innovators have done: elevate yourself from uninspired, early works to creations that change the world.

Myth Five: Creativity Comes From Chilling Out

Relaxing is important for kickstarting creativity. But only if that relaxing is a specific kind: relaxing logic. By relaxing logic, you free your brain's deep imagination hub—the default mode network—to start speculating new plans and plots. That speculating can be fun, because it's unconstrained by prior rules, making it the mental essence of liberty. But like liberty, it's not free. It requires work. So, discipline yourself with the exercises in this book.

Myth Six: Creativity is Harmonious

What's harmonious is logic. Logic is universal, unified, and balanced. And also, the opposite of creativity. Creativity is specific, individual, and challenging. And it's born not from harmony, but from tension, struggle, and conflict: tension with the environment, struggle against the past, and conflict with others. That conflict can break out into open war, as in the primordial cauldron of nature. Or, it can be managed, as in creative industries. But it always carries an edge—and that edge must be embraced. Don't fear the creative fight. Lean into it.

Myth Seven: Creativity is Going Rogue

Creativity challenges compliance—but it challenges compliance to make compliance better. That's because creativity shares compliance's core mission: life. Like compliance, creativity's purpose is to help us survive and thrive. When creativity tests compliance, it therefore does so to *strengthen* and *update* compliance by anticipating potential cracks and gaps in standard operative procedures. As long as those procedures are working, true creatives follow them. And when those procedures break down under the changing pressures of life, true creatives maintain compliance's original spirit through the invention of new standard operating procedures that preserve life and promote it.

Myth Eight: Creativity is Totally Original

Nothing creative is totally original. Like everything biological, it always inherits something from the past. And a great many effective innovations aren't very original at all. They're clever tweaks or adjustments to existing tactics or technologies, adapting them ingeniously to new challenges and opportunities. So, don't fall into the trap of thinking that a breakthrough has to be radically unprecedented. The definition of an innovation is simply: something new that works. And things are often more likely to work if they plug in, at least partially, to existing systems.

Myth Nine: Creativity Comes From Within

Creativity is a learned skill, improved by studying the successful innovations of nature and other creators. Creativity is fed by dynamic conflict with outside actors and environments. And creativity is scaled by teams working to link their imaginations together. So, no: creativity doesn't come from within. It is a gift inherited—and a gift grown by turning outward.

Myth Ten: Creativity is Optional

Creativity is the reason that our species exists—and the source of the tools that now keep us alive. Without creativity, we will not endure, and neither will the things we care about. We cannot pass the task of creativity onto computers and their Artificial Intelligence; computers are capable only of logic, not of invention. So, if you shirk the call to creativity, we will lose life's next great battle— and eventually, the war.

Coda: The End of War

He was the real life Willy Wonka. But before he could build his chocolate wonderland, he had to stop the bombs from falling.

His name was Egbert Cadbury. He was an Englishman born in 1893 to a family of Quaker pacifists. But when war broke out against Germany, he felt compelled to quit college and enlist.

Through a mixture of bravery and luck, Cadbury became a pilot. And in 1915, he was handed what appeared a hopeless mission: shoot down the Zeppelins.

The Zeppelins were a strange and terrible innovation: massive airships that floated silent through the night to rain fire on the sleeping homes below. They sparked horror in England. And they offered a glimpse of a nightmare future: death dropped quiet from the sky by machines unseen.

Defeating this nightmare future was essential. As long as the Zeppelins ruled the atmosphere, there could no peace, only terror. Yet to defeat them was apparently unachievable. For fifteen months, Cadbury courageously piloted a rickety biplane against fleets of Zeppelins, with no success. Bullets fired from below were useless, as were bombs dropped from above. Moving Cadbury to vent to his brother that the whole thing was stupid. Men would die; the Zeppelins would continue to fly; and nothing would change.

But then came the night of 27 November 1916. That night, a Zeppelin flew past Cadbury's air station. The Zeppelin had already brushed off half-a-dozen aircraft. But Cadbury took after it in a plane equipped with a recently invented technology: guns loaded with tracer-explosive bullets, some of them literally packed with dynamite. And although those bullets had yet to produce results for Cadbury and his squadron mates, Cadbury had meditated on their past failures and hatched a fresh strategy.

Previously, Cadbury had done the usual thing of flying perpendicular to the Zeppelin, giving his guns the biggest target to hit. Yet now, he would try firing in parallel, raking bullets down the airship's vast length. So, he swung up behind the Zeppelin, pumping his dynamite ammo into its stern.

At first, nothing happened. But suddenly, a flame sparked inside the floating behemoth. And then in a flash, the whole airship combusted in fire, tumbling with a horrid shriek into the sea.

For this inventive feat, Cadbury was promoted to major and placed in charge of his squadron. In his new position, he trained dozens of pilots in his Zeppelin-hunting method. Until in mid-1918, the Zeppelins struck back.

The strike was engineered by the Zeppelin Fuhrer, Peter Strasser. Strasser had instituted a new bombing program, aimed directly at civilians. As he grimly put it: "There's no such creature as a noncombatant. Modern warfare is total."

To power this total war, Strasser ordered the construction of a new kind of Zeppelin: the X-Class, or Super Zeppelin. It bristled with heavy machine guns and could drop 3 tons of bombs: the same as a World War II Flying Fortress.

On 5 August 1918, Strasser took command of this innovation and ordered it into the air. A few hours later, Cadbury was attending a charity concert when he got the news: the Super Zeppelin was attacking. Abandoning the concert, Cadbury raced to his airfield, where he found only one operational flyer: an Airco reconnaissance bomber, later to become famous in the United States as a mail-delivery plane.

Wrestling the bulky biplane skyward, Cadbury powered through the enveloping night, spotting the Fuhrer and his Super Zeppelin over the sea, bombs undropped. The Super Zeppelin was thousands of feet overhead, as Cadbury later remembered: "It was a most fascinating sight—awe inspiring—to see [it] blotting the whole sky above."

Rapidly adjusting his tactics, Cadbury jettisoned fuel to gain altitude—then hit the Super Zeppelin with a parallel gun burst down its port side. Out of the sky the monster fell, filling Cadbury with an expected feeling of relief—and an unexpected feeling of horror: "It was one of the most terrifying sights I have ever seen to see this huge machine hurtling down with all those crew on board."

For his triumph, Cadbury was knighted. And he remained, for his entire life, a war hero. But his memory of war was not happy. He confessed to his brother that all he could remember when he shut his eyes was the Zeppelin's thirty screaming crew members as they dropped on fire from the sky. All he could see was their raw panic as the airship's fabric combusted and they realized that they were about to fall, helpless, to death.

This flashback vision of horror was the other face of Cadbury's creative imagination. The same perspective-taking neural circuits that had helped Cadbury attack the Zeppelin from an inventive new angle, yielding his unprecedented victory, had now leaped him into the mind of his defeated enemy. And inside that conquered mind, Cadbury realized: it would have been better if the Super Zeppelin had never been conceived. It would have been better if the airship Fuhrer had never hatched his new bombing doctrine. It would have been better if the whole war had never been fought.

After the war, Cadbury continued being an innovator. He took over his family chocolate business and turned it into a new kind of factory, with playgrounds and athletic fields. He sold delicious, original confections: the flake, the creme egg, the fruit & nut bar. He brought down manufacturing costs, transforming chocolate from a luxury item to an everyday treat. The same ingenious brain that had out-innovated the innovations of the Zeppelin Fuhrer now created millions of daily smiles, across the globe.

Such are creativity's two great wonders: to win the war and burnish the peace. And yet these two wonders aren't creativity's most important job. As Cadbury realized when he imagined his way into the minds of the Zeppelin men who'd died, creativity's most important job is to prevent war in the first place.

War is the failure of more creative efforts at conflict-resolution. War is giving up on humanity and resorting to force.

War cannot always be avoided. And when it cannot, creative strategy is the way to end it quickly.

But the better way to end war is to devote creativity to anticipating conflict, stopping the horror before it begins.

Final Review

Intelligence = Logic + Creativity

Creativity = Perspective-Taking + Plot-Twisting

Perspective-Taking = Self-Distancing + Other Why

Self-Distancing = Exiting your hopes and fears

Other Why = The rationale for another person's plans or actions

Plot-Twisting = Exceptional Information + Causal Reasoning

Exceptional Information = Data not predicted by existing rules

Causal Reasoning = Speculating from causes to effects

No creative idea can ever be Right or True.

It can only be testable.

So, test it fast.

Toggle on Creativity: When Asymmetric Conflict and
                         Uncertainty increase

    Toggle on Logic: When Equilibrium is restored and
                         Stability extends

The Circle of Creativity:

Creativity → Innovation → Compliance

Limits of Compliance → Strife → Creativity

The Innovator's Mantra:

Want it, Get it. Risk it, Win it.

Acknowledgments

Lt. Col. Kenneth Long, for being the Catalyst.

Lt. Col. Richard McConnell, for being the Sage.

Lt. Col. Jacob Mong, for being the Engine.

Maj. Angela Samosorn for being the Pioneer.

Col. Thomas A. Shoffner, for being the Leader.

Prof. Greg Bunch, for being the Prophet.

And Sgt. Jones and the other Quantico 96 instructors, for being the Teacher. *"Fletcher, you a doggone miracle, you know that? How else that little neck be holding up that giant head?"*

Made in the USA
Monee, IL
07 December 2022

19972329R10059